MEDITATION

—— AND ——

CONTEMPLATION

Other Books by the Author

THE EXAMEN PRAYER
Ignatian Wisdom for Our Lives Today

THE DISCERNMENT OF SPIRITS
An Ignatian Guide for Everyday Living

SPIRITUAL CONSOLATION
An Ignatian Guide for the Greater Discernment of Spirits

AN IGNATIAN INTRODUCTION TO PRAYER
Scriptural Reflections According to the Spiritual Exercises

MEDITATION

—— AND ——

CONTEMPLATION

An Ignatian Guide
to Praying with Scripture

Timothy M. Gallagher, O.M.V.

A Crossroad Book
The Crossroad Publishing Company
New York

The Crossroad Publishing Company
www.CrossroadPublishing.com

© 2008 by Timothy M. Gallagher, O.M.V.

Printed in the United States of America.

The text of this book is set in 12/15.5 Sabon. The display face is Tiepolo.

Cataloging-in-Publication Data is available from
the Library of Congress

ISBN-10: 0-8245-2488-8
ISBN-13: 978-0-8245-2488-3

5   6   7   8   9   10   12   11

Contents

Acknowledgments   7

Introduction   9

Outline of Meditation and Contemplation   15

1. "What I Wish and Desire"   19

    "These Cleansing Tears" / 19
    "I Let Those Words Swim in My Heart" / 22

2. The Body of the Prayer: Meditation   27

    A Threefold Process / 27
    "I Opened the Epistles of St. Paul" / 29
    "Do Not Be Afraid" / 33

3. The Body of the Prayer: Contemplation   35

    A Threefold Process / 35
    How Do I Know It Is Not Just My Imagination? / 36
    "I Took the Place of Zacchaeus" / 38
    "Let the Children Come to Me" / 39
    Can I Pray This Way? / 40
    The Body of the Prayer: Meditation and
       Contemplation / 44

4. Before the Prayer Begins   47

    "My Heart Is Ready, O God" / 47
    Preparing for Prayer / 53

5. Beginning the Prayer   55

    When Heart Speaks to Heart / 55
    "I Will Consider How God Our Lord Looks
       upon Me" / 57

I Offer All My Will and Actions to God
    (Preparatory Prayer) / 59
I Review the Scripture for This Prayer / 61
I Imaginatively Enter the Place of This Scripture
    (Composition) / 62
I Ask of God What I Wish and Desire in This Prayer / 64
How Do I Use These Spiritual Tools? / 66

6. Ending the Prayer   68

The Rhythms of the Heart / 68
I Speak to God as My Heart Is Moved (Colloquy) / 69
I Conclude with an Our Father / 72
Reviewing Our Prayer / 73

7. Further Counsels for Prayer   77

"To Find More Readily What One Desires" / 77
Prayer and the Body / 78
"There I Will Rest" / 79
Struggles in Prayer / 80
Growth in Prayer / 83
Accompaniment in Prayer / 85

8. Putting It All Together: An Example   88

The Elements of a Flexible Whole / 88
First Day / 89
Second Day / 91
Third Day / 91
The Following Days / 91
In the Creativity of the Spirit / 92

9. The Fruits of Prayer   94

What Will Happen If I Pray This Way? / 94
"A Pure Gift of Grace" / 98

Notes   101

Acknowledgments

I am deeply grateful to the many people whose assistance made the writing of this book possible: to Joseph Schner, S.J., the Jesuit community of Pedro Arrupe House, and the faculty and staff of Regis College, Toronto, who offered me warm hospitality and unfailing support during the writing of this book; to Claire-Marie Hart for her generous and expert editing; to Carol McGinness for her invaluable assistance with word processing and permissions; and to William Brown, O.M.V., my provincial, for his personal encouragement and for providing this time of writing.

I thank, too, those who accompanied me with their counsel prior to the writing and their reflections on the manuscript during the writing itself: George Aschenbrenner, S.J., Susan Dumas, Harvey Egan, S.J., Theresa Galvan, C.N.D., Gill Goulding, C.J., Elizabeth Koessler, Catherine Macaulay, Gertrude Mahoney, S.N.D., Edward O'Flaherty, S.J., Germana Santos, F.S.P., Ernest Sherstone, O.M.V., Al Starkey, and Robert Uzziglio. Their support and insights were a treasured resource during those months.

Finally, I thank the following for permission to reprint copyrighted material:

Introduction

My first exposure to meditation came through St. Francis de Sales. For years I had heard of meditation and had seen it recommended in spiritual books. It appeared that this form of prayer was a source of great blessing, and my interest was awakened. Yet I found no way to learn about meditation. It was inviting but also mysterious. I never imagined that it could apply to me, an ordinary Christian.

Then I read Francis de Sales's *Introduction to the Devout Life*. There I discovered ten meditations outlined for beginners. At the time, I did not know that Francis had experienced the Spiritual Exercises of St. Ignatius of Loyola and learned much from them. I only knew that I had, for the first time, found a path toward meditation.

I made Francis de Sales's ten meditations and liked the experience. When I completed the tenth, however, I was at a loss once more. This had been a welcome first step. Yet I had no idea how to continue and did not know where to find further guidance.

Years later, during my seminary training, I learned more about meditation. My companions and I were taught how to meditate, and we practiced this daily. We were grateful for this help. Meditation no longer seemed a remote and mysterious reality.

Several years later, I made the Spiritual Exercises of St. Ignatius. Day after day in the retreat, the director explained Ignatius's counsels on prayer. We put those counsels into practice and, in personal meetings with the director, found answers to our questions. When the retreat ended, I thought, "Someone has finally taught me to pray." Gratitude for Ignatius of Loyola's teaching on prayer arose within me — a gratitude that since then has only deepened. Ignatius's clear and practical counsels opened for me, as for so many before me, a sure path of prayer.

After my seminary years, I began sharing this teaching in retreats and watched this same experience repeat itself. Again and again I witnessed the spiritual energy awakened by Ignatius's teaching on prayer. Through it, desire for prayer, inhibited by uncertainty, is *set free,* and a clear path opens toward prayer. The purpose of this book is to share that teaching.

Our focus will be the two basic Ignatian methods for prayer with Scripture: *meditation,* the reflective approach, and *contemplation,* the imaginative approach. Both methods, through different human capabilities — our ability to reflect on the meaning of the text and our ability to enter the scene in the text imaginatively — open for us the message of the Scriptures. Through different gateways, both lead to the heart.

I choose these two methods because they are Ignatius's starting point for prayer with Scripture. Other methods of prayer build upon them, but these two are foundational. This choice also permits us to explore both methods deeply in a limited number of pages. The clarity that emerges is invaluable. It allows a solidly grounded use of these methods, with flexibility, as the Spirit draws us individually. Such freedom contributes greatly to fruitful prayer with Scripture.

My approach to Ignatius's teaching on meditation and contemplation is based upon two convictions. The first is that the best way to understand this teaching is to examine what Ignatius actually says in his *Spiritual Exercises:* to allow Ignatius himself, through his own words, to teach

> Both terms, *meditation* and *contemplation*, are used in widely varying senses today. For Ignatius, they have the specific meaning briefly indicated here and elaborated throughout this book. Both presuppose Christian revelation. Within Christian tradition, Ignatius's use of *contemplation* differs from that of John of the Cross. For John, contemplation signifies infused, passive, mystical prayer. For Ignatius, the same word indicates active imaginative participation in a Gospel event.

these methods. Direct contact with his words opens for us the full richness and endless freshness of this teaching.[1]

The second is that teaching about prayer comes alive when presented through experience. Experience gives life to the written text and reveals its applicability for our prayer today. In this book, consequently, we will consistently illustrate Ignatius's teaching through experience.

Some of these experiences are found in written sources. Most, however, I have taken from personal interviews. These people shared their experiences of meditation and contemplation and gave me explicit permission to quote their words. I have done so respecting their confidentiality. Thus I refer to them either without proper names ("a man says," "a woman says") or with a proper name other than their own. The examples given, therefore, all describe real experiences.[2]

These persons represent many vocations. Some are priests, some religious. Most are lay people. Some have prayed with Scripture for years; others have begun only recently. All live in ordinary circumstances according to their respective vocations: family, community, professional work, ministry. All have grown to love prayer with Scripture. I am deeply grateful to these persons; their sharing constitutes the richest part of this book.

This book is for all who desire to pray with Scripture. It is for those who have never prayed with Scripture and wish to begin. It is for those who have tried to pray with Scripture but have encountered difficulties. It is for those who pray with Scripture and seek renewal in this practice. It is for spiritual directors, retreat directors, and all who teach prayer with Scripture. In all these settings, Ignatius has effective counsels to offer.

I begin this book with outlines of meditation and contemplation. These outlines contain all the elements of both Ignatian methods. The book then examines these elements, first as individual steps and then as a flexible whole.

A first chapter highlights the *desire* that motivates prayer with Scripture. The next chapters clarify the *central intuition* of these methods: reflective (meditative) and imaginative (contemplative) entry into the Scripture. Subsequent chapters consider Ignatius's counsels on *preparing, beginning,* and *ending* the prayer. The concluding chapters portray these elements as a *whole* and describe their *fruits.*

Obviously, much more than this can be said about prayer. This book has one essential purpose: to present in a clear and usable way two Ignatian methods for prayer with Scripture. Further questions may emerge as prayer with Scripture unfolds and the individual's practice of prayer deepens. If so, counsel will then be sought. The gift of these methods is to ensure that, by charting a wise course from the start, this prayer will faithfully lead to such growth.

The interviews were often a moving experience. In those conversations we walked on holy ground. I marveled at how creatively the Spirit works through reflective and imaginative prayer with Scripture. I understood in a new way how effectively these methods respond to the deepest needs of our hearts at prayer. I felt a new sense of hope as story after story revealed God's transforming grace at work in our world.

Ignatius has much to teach us about prayer. In this book we will explore that teaching and the richness of growth it offers.

Outline of Meditation
and Contemplation

On the following two pages I provide the classic outlines of Ignatian meditation and contemplation. These outlines reproduce the steps as described in the *Spiritual Exercises*. Ignatius generally employs the first person singular ("I will consider . . . ") in describing these steps; I have extended this use to the entire method. At key points I have included traditional vocabulary in parentheses.

MEDITATION

"I will consider how God our Lord looks upon me."

I offer all my will and actions to God *(preparatory prayer).*
I review the Scripture for this prayer.
I imaginatively enter the place of this Scripture *(composition).*
I ask of God what I wish and desire in this prayer.

Body of the Prayer. For each point,

    I call to mind this truth, with love.

    I ponder it, with love.

    I embrace it, with love and desire.

I speak to God as my heart is moved *(colloquy).*
I conclude with an *Our Father.*

CONTEMPLATION

"I will consider how God our Lord looks upon me."

I offer all my will and actions to God *(preparatory prayer)*.

I review the Scripture for this prayer.

I imaginatively enter the place of this Scripture *(composition)*.

I ask of God what I wish and desire in this prayer.

Body of the Prayer. For each point,

> I see the persons.
>
> I hear the words.
>
> I observe the actions.

I speak to God as my heart is moved *(colloquy)*.

I conclude with an *Our Father*.

Chapter One

"What I Wish and Desire"

Make a little time for God and rest a while in him....
Speak now to God and say with your whole heart: "I
seek your face; your face, Lord, I desire."

— St. Anselm

"These Cleansing Tears"

A woman was ready to pray. These were days of retreat
dedicated to prayer with Scripture. This day she felt drawn
to pray with the trial of Jesus. She writes:

The scene came alive in my imagination and my heart.
I saw Jesus standing before Pontius Pilate and his accusers. *How could Jesus stand there while everyone*
called for his death, I wondered. *How could he be so*
calm? As I placed myself completely into that scene,
feeling Jesus' calmness, I began to hear Jesus saying
quietly to the crowd, "Yes. Take me. Do what you want
with me, for my death will be your salvation." I could
see the Father hugging him tightly. "Give yourself over
to them," God told his Son. "I can never let you go, no
matter what happens. I am with you. You are safe in
my arms." After a long period of prayer, I realized that
the Father was within me as he was within Jesus. He
was also holding me: "Do not be afraid. You are safe
in my arms."[3]

19

Seventeen years earlier, this woman, Kathryn, had been admitted to a hospital for a simple outpatient surgery. She was young, healthy, strong, and capable. Soon after the surgery, however, something went terribly wrong. Four days later, she learned that she had suffered a stroke. Years of struggle with severe physical and emotional disabilities followed. Kathryn strove to cope with these disabilities and her efforts were, in some measure, successful. Yet deeper struggles remained. Now grace was about to touch that deeper level.

Kathryn continued her prayer:

> On another day, I contemplated Jesus right after Pilate had condemned him to death and washed his hands of the whole affair. I saw Jesus dragged off by those who wanted him dead. The moment of terror I felt, as his final walk through Jerusalem began, was excruciating. I prayed many hours, holding that terror in my heart, desiring to comfort Jesus, to tell him I was there for him and that I would not leave him alone.

Kathryn shares Jesus' final walk through Jerusalem in deep communion with him. She desires "to comfort Jesus, to tell him I was there for him and that I would not leave him alone." Kathryn draws close to Jesus as she prays.

Her prayer deepens further:

> One day in prayer, I stood beneath the cross and sank to the ground at its foot after he had died. I had told Jesus I would not leave him alone, and so I stayed there keeping watch. I kept the cross before my eyes for hours, feeling the sorrow Mary must have felt, as I asked for the courage to stay near the cross. It was at this point that my retreat director pointed out to me that perhaps God was bringing together Jesus' experience and

my own. I began to cry when I returned to prayer. For several hours, in prayer...scenes of my hospital stay after my stroke so many years before alternated with scenes of Jesus' passion and death. It was like watching a movie. My moments of loneliness and fear alternated with Jesus' loneliness and fear. I cried inconsolably for hours — seventeen years worth of tears. God was truly embracing me tightly and saying, "Do not be afraid even of this. I am holding you tightly and nothing can hurt you."

Kathryn describes the fruit of those blessed hours:

These cleansing tears began a process of healing, a miracle of God's love for me as I began to pray over my "passion." Just as I, in that prayer, had remained beneath the cross after Jesus had died, I now saw Jesus sitting on the floor at the foot of my hospital bed keeping *me* company. As I had stayed with Jesus, he now kept watch with me. The many lonely years of struggling with the consequences of my stroke... were "healed" in this prayer....I began to see that though I had kept myself at a sufficient distance from God to protect myself from anything else God could "do" to me, God nevertheless had waited until the right moment to "seize me by the arms" and turn me toward him.

The eye of faith clearly perceives the authenticity and richness of this prayer. Before it, we simply stand in wonder and praise. These "cleansing tears" begin a process of healing that Kathryn, after years of helpless struggle, knows to be a miracle of God's love. Her prayer with Jesus' passion leads, by God's loving gift, to a healing in her own "passion."

Kathryn tells us that, as she prayed with Jesus' passion, "the scene came alive in my imagination and my heart." She hears Jesus speak. She experiences the Father's loving presence to Jesus and his loving presence to her. She shares with Jesus his final walk through Jerusalem. She stands beneath the cross and accompanies Jesus in his final hours. Her own passion alternates with Jesus' passion, is enlightened by Jesus' passion, and is healed by Jesus' passion. She sees Jesus keeping watch with her in her hospital room...and cleansing tears begin to fall.

Is such freedom possible in praying with Scripture? Can we too be present to a Gospel scene and live it from within in this way? Is such prayer open to all? Is it possible for everyone? Is it possible *for me?* These are fundamental questions for prayer, and much depends upon the answers to them.

"I Let Those Words Swim in My Heart"

Mark was baptized as an adult eight years ago, and his baptism began a quest for communion with God. He says:

> During these years, I learned various ways of praying. I knew that the Scriptures were the Word of God and I knew that people had reverence for them. But, for me, they were just written words. I never really sank into them the way I could with a novel, for example. I always stayed on the surface. I heard the Scriptures proclaimed but I didn't really experience them.

Seven years after his baptism, Mark joined a group that shared his spiritual quest. One evening, the group prayed with Matthew 8:23–27, Jesus' calming of the storm at sea. The leader encouraged the members to quiet their hearts. Then he slowly read the passage, out loud, three times. He invited them to enter the scene imaginatively — to see, hear, and share in the events of the Gospel text: the rising of the storm, the fear of the disciples in the boat, their desperate cry to Jesus, his calming of the storm, and Jesus' invitation to faith. Mark recounts his experience:

> It was a revolution. It opened a new world for me. I had felt as though I had God figured out, somehow, but I hadn't been able to get close to Jesus. That evening, the Scripture came alive. I'd been passive, outside of it. It had just been a story. When I prayed in this way, I no longer felt like I was outside the story; I was *in* the story. I could do more than just imagine Peter in the boat, for example; I could actually look Peter in the eyes. I could be one of the characters and follow the story from within. I was in the story, but not so bound by it that I couldn't ask something of Jesus or of Peter. And I realized that Jesus was not as far away as I thought. I found myself marveling at how near he was to me. I'm still amazed by this experience, still in awe of it.

He continues:

> It took me eight years of really seeking Christ to find this way of praying. Now, when I hear the Gospel proclaimed at Mass, I'm there in the scene; I'm not passive anymore. And if you *experience* something, you remember the details. If I just read something, I remember maybe 10 percent of it. But when I experience something, like the calming of the storm, then I remember it with all the details — even, for example, the pillow under Jesus' head as he sleeps in the boat. I try to do this now every time I'm at Mass. Sometimes it's easier, and sometimes it's harder.

Mark goes on to give another example:

A few months ago, I was praying with Mary's response to the angel in Luke 1:38: "Behold, I am the hand-maid of the Lord. May it be done to me according to your word." It was a beautiful experience. Those words stayed with me throughout the whole day and still re-main with me. They give me a greater ability to make choices for God in daily situations. In a certain situ-ation, for example, I may want to do something, but I sense that the Lord wants something else. It may be something simple, whether I should take a moment to help a person who is assisting me with a project. And I'll hear the words, "May it be done to me according to your word." That helps me take the time to meet the other person's needs.

On another day, Mark prayed with the passage about Jesus as the Good Shepherd in John 10. He describes his experience:

It was a beautiful time of prayer, an intimate time. There was so much in the words; it's so beautifully written. I wasn't reading words; it was alive, almost directly touching my heart. I had read this text many times, and it hadn't really spoken to me. The words had just lain there on the page. For some reason, this time I had a deep sense of Christ, of awe, of the Good Shepherd easing my fears, and leading me.

This time of prayer was more meditative and not so much in the imagination. I let those beautiful words sort of swim in my heart, back and forth. That prayer left me spiritually happy, kind of on a high for a day and a half. I couldn't stop thinking about those words. I used them in some teaching I was doing, and I knew that it wasn't just teaching; I was teaching from the heart, from experience.

Like Kathryn, Mark experiences the power of praying with the Gospel through active presence to the scene. This way of praying is a revolution for him; it opens "a new world" for him. Through it, the Scriptures come alive for him in a new way. Mark no longer feels passive with respect to the Scriptures, somehow outside the events. Now he can interact with the people in the scene. He can live the Gospel event "from within." With a sense of marvel, Mark realizes as he prays that Jesus is "not as far away as I thought"; he discovers how near Jesus is to him. Even a year later, Mark is "still amazed by this experience."

We may note Mark's awareness that at times his prayer with Scripture is more imaginative, at times more reflective. When he prays with the calming of the storm, for example, he is "in the story" — he can "look Peter in the eyes," can "ask something of Jesus or of Peter." He experiences the calming of the storm and can remember its many details. Here the *imaginative* element is predominant.

When, however, Mark prays with the passage of the Good Shepherd, the words themselves of the text capture his heart. The words are "alive," and "almost directly" touch his heart. Mark lets "those beautiful words sort of swim" in his heart, "back and forth." In the following days, he cannot "stop thinking about those words." As he himself was perceptive enough to note, "This time of prayer was more meditative and not so much in the imagination." Here the *reflective* element is predominant.

Clearly, both ways of praying are fruitful for Mark. He appears at ease with both, ready to pray in either way, flexibly, as he feels moved that day.

Again, as with Kathryn's experience, the person of faith cannot doubt the authenticity of Mark's prayer. Again the same questions arise: Do we, too, have this freedom in praying with Scripture? Can we be present to a Gospel scene and live it from within in this way? Are both the imaginative and reflective approaches open to all? Is such prayer possible for all? Is it possible for me? If so, how can I begin such prayer with Scripture? And how can I grow in such prayer?

To the human heart that cries out to God with St. Anselm, "I seek your face; your face, Lord, I desire," these questions matter deeply. When this quest for God is, as Ignatius says, "what I wish and desire," then our hearts thirst for answers to these questions. Now, with Ignatius himself as our guide, we will search for these answers.

Chapter Two

The Body of the Prayer: Meditation

Do you want to know what our Lord meant in all this?
Learn it well: love was what he meant. Who showed it
to you? Love. What did he show you? Love. Why did
he show it? Out of love. — Julian of Norwich

A Threefold Process

When Mark prayed with the passage of the Good Shepherd
(John 10:1–18), he tells us that the words were "alive," "almost directly touching my heart," and continues, "I let those
beautiful words sort of swim in my heart, back and forth."
Mark describes an unhurried, happy, faith-filled reflection
on the words of the Scripture, with profound awareness of
the Lord's presence. As these words "swim" in his heart and
he ponders them again and again, he is aware that Christ is
saying these words *now,* to *him:* "I had a deep sense...of
the Good Shepherd easing *my* fears, and leading *me.*" His
heart delights in these beautiful words, feels a sense of awe,
and is made "spiritually happy" in the ensuing days.

In Ignatius's vocabulary, such loving reflection on revealed
truth is *meditation* — the *reflective* process by which we
enter the richness of God's Word and hear that Word as
spoken personally to us today. Ignatius describes meditation
as prayer "with the three powers" (memory, understanding,
will).[4] We begin by *calling to mind* this word. (Mark reads

the text: "I am the good shepherd. . . . I know mine and mine know me. . . . I will lay down my life for the sheep.") We then *ponder* its meaning. (Mark reflects with affectionate wonder on Jesus as the Good Shepherd who accompanies him, leads him, and eases his fears.) As the meaning of these truths is revealed to us, our hearts *embrace* this meaning with love and desire. (Mark feels a "deep sense of Christ," of loving awe, and his heart welcomes the Good Shepherd who eases his fears and leads him.)

With Ignatius, we may outline the natural unfolding of this process in the following way. When I turn to the Scripture I have chosen, I find there a number of revealed truths (in Mark's prayer, for example, that Christ is the Good Shepherd, that he knows his own, that he lays down his life for them). As my heart is drawn to one of these truths,

- I *call to mind* this truth, with love

- I *ponder* it, with love

- I *embrace* it, with love and desire

This process by which I call to mind, ponder, and embrace successive truths in a scriptural text is Ignatian *meditation*. Ignatius's description of this threefold process simply articulates what we do naturally when we reflect on God's Word with faith and receptive hearts. A conscious grasp of the human structure of this process, however, permits us to meditate with greater understanding, and so with greater confidence. Knowledge of this structure also assists us in times of distraction: it is a solid starting point to which we can always return. Some examples will further solidify our understanding of this process.

"I Opened the Epistles of St. Paul"

A classic text in the writings of St. Thérèse of Lisieux provides a rich illustration of this threefold process. Thérèse describes a day when she prayed with 1 Corinthians 12–13. She tells us that she was led to this text through an experience of conflicting desires. As she prayed, she poured out these desires to the Lord:

> To be Your *Spouse,* to be a *Carmelite,* and by my union with You to be the *Mother* of souls, should this not suffice me? And yet it is not so. No doubt, these three privileges sum up my true *vocation: Carmelite, Spouse, Mother,* and yet I feel within me other *vocations.* I feel the vocation of the WARRIOR, THE PRIEST, THE APOSTLE, THE DOCTOR, THE MARTYR. Finally, I feel the need and desire of carrying out the most heroic deeds for *You, O Jesus....* O Jesus, my Love, my Life, how can I combine these contrasts? How can I realize the desires of my poor *little soul?*[5]

The yearnings of her heart led this woman of God to the Scriptures:

> During my meditation, my desires caused me a veritable martyrdom, and I opened the Epistles of St. Paul to find some kind of answer. Chapters 12 and 13 of the First Epistle to the Corinthians fell under my eyes. I read there, in the first of these chapters, that *all* cannot be apostles, prophets, doctors, etc., that the Church is composed of different members, and that the eye cannot be the hand *at one and the same time.* The answer was clear, but it did not fulfill my desires and gave me no peace.

Thérèse had found a first but still unsatisfying answer to her yearnings. She persevered in her prayer, reading further in 1 Corinthians:

> Without becoming discouraged, I continued my reading, and this sentence consoled me: "*Yet strive after THE BETTER GIFTS, and I point out to you a yet more excellent way.*" And the Apostle explains how all *the most PERFECT gifts* are nothing without *LOVE. That Charity is the EXCELLENT WAY that leads most surely* to God.

Now Thérèse had found her complete answer. She writes:

> I finally had rest. Considering the mystical body of the Church, I had not recognized myself in any of the members described by St. Paul, or rather I had desired to see myself in them *all. Charity* gave me the key to my *vocation.* I understood that if the Church had a body composed of different members, the most necessary and most noble of all could not be lacking to it, and so I understood that the Church *had a Heart and that this Heart was BURNING WITH LOVE. I understood that it was Love alone* that made the Church's members act, that if *Love* ever became extinct, apostles would not preach the Gospel and martyrs would not shed their blood. I understood that LOVE COMPRISED ALL VOCATIONS, THAT LOVE WAS EVERYTHING, THAT IT EMBRACED ALL TIMES AND PLACES....IN A WORD, THAT IT WAS ETERNAL!

As Thérèse grasped the full answer to her longings, her heart responded with joy:

Then, in the excess of my delirious joy, I cried out: O Jesus, my Love...my *vocation*, at last I have found it....MY VOCATION IS LOVE!

Yes, I have found my place in the Church and it is You, O my God, who have given me this place; in the heart of the Church, my Mother, I shall be *Love*. Thus I shall be everything, and thus my dream will be realized.

Why speak of delirious joy? No, this expression is not exact, for it was rather the calm and serene peace of the navigator perceiving the beacon which must lead him to the port....O luminous Beacon of love, I know how to reach You, I have found the secret of possessing your flame.

With reverence for the grace at work in Thérèse's prayer, we will explore this account in the light of Ignatius's description of meditation. This prayer, as all true prayer, begins with *desire:* "How can I realize *the desires* of my poor little soul?"[6] This desire leads Thérèse to pray with Scripture. She turns to the Letters of St. Paul, and finds herself drawn to 1 Corinthians 12–13. With unerring spiritual instinct, she follows the drawings of her heart and prays with this text.

Thérèse's first step in prayer is to *call to mind* the truths contained in this Scripture. She does this through attentive reading of the text: "In my prayer...*I opened* the Epistles of St. Paul....Chapters 12 and 13 of the First Epistle to the Corinthians fell under my eyes. *I read* there....Without becoming discouraged, *I continued my reading....*" Her attentive and faith-filled reading of the Scripture renders its content profoundly present to Thérèse and prepares the subsequent steps in her prayer.

Having read the text, she then *ponders* the truths it contains, and her understanding grows: "The *answer* was clear.

...*Considering* the mystical body of the Church.... I *under-stood* that if the Church had a body...I *understood* that the Church had a Heart.... My vocation, at last I *have found* it.... Yes, I *have found* my place in the Church....I *know how* to reach You, I *have found* the secret." The richness of such pondering is strikingly evident in Thérèse's experience. God's grace mingles with human reflection, and the heart finds answers to its longings.

We may note that Thérèse does not attempt to focus on the entire text at once, but calls to mind and ponders successive sections of the text. In Ignatius's vocabulary, she ponders successive *points* in the text.[7] By praying with smaller sections in the text, she is more easily able to assimilate the whole.

Now that its meaning has spoken deeply to her heart, Thérèse *embraces* this teaching with love and desire: "This sentence *consoled* me....I finally had *rest*.... Then, in the excess of my delirious *joy*, I cried out....No, this expression is not exact, for it was rather the *calm and serene peace* of the navigator perceiving the beacon which must lead him to the port." What Thérèse has called to mind, and what her understanding has grasped, she now embraces with all the love and desire of her heart. Her meditation has reached its deep center: through the Scriptures, God has spoken to Thérèse's heart, and Thérèse has responded from her heart.

Evidently, Thérèse does not move by conscious decision from one step to the next — first calling to mind the truths in the text, then pondering them, then embracing them. Rather, this movement simply occurs according to a natural human process. In fact, as she meditates, these steps succeed one another in an ongoing process. Such is the normal pattern of meditation.

"Do Not Be Afraid"

Dan describes an experience of praying with Luke 5:1–11, the miraculous catch of fish. He remembers this as a powerful time of prayer. He says:

> As I read this Gospel, Peter's words to Jesus after the catch of fish really captured me. He said, "Depart from me, Lord, for I am a sinful man." What struck me was not that Peter was so humble that he said this to Jesus. It was something else, and it has never left me since that day. Whenever I am discouraged, I say the opposite: "Lord, I'm a sinner. Do not depart from me." I thought of the spiritual boldness of St. Thérèse, who said to the Lord, "*Because* I am a sinner, do not depart from me." I often return to that day when I was seized by the thought that, whatever my sinfulness or folly, I would never say to Jesus, "Depart from me," but always, "Stay!"
>
> I saw Peter as a typical man. He was humbled, and that is not easy for a man. He was brought to his knees, and I understood him as saying, "I'm useless." Men want to be doing, want to be in control, and Peter, when he brought in all those fish, realized that he was not in control. What he was saying was this: I can't handle this; I don't know how to deal with this, so you will have to depart from me. Jesus simply says to him, "Do not be afraid."

Dan continues:

> Jesus saw the whole picture. He saw all that would happen to Peter in the future. And Jesus was saying to him, "I've let this happen to show you that without me you can do nothing, but that, with me, your life will be greatly fruitful. Through my power you will see

much greater things than this catch of fish." It seemed to me that this dialogue reflected Jesus and every man. Once we realize that we are not in control, we want the situation to disappear. And Jesus doesn't do this. He shows us what he showed Peter: that with him our lives will be very fruitful. And so I don't want Jesus to go.

Again we stand on holy ground. With reverence, we will review this experience for the learning about prayer it affords.

The *reflective* approach is evident in Dan's prayer; this is an experience of *meditation.* Dan does not speak of imagining the scene. While such imagining may be present to some degree, his primary focus appears to be *the meaning of specific words* in the text: the dialogue between Peter ("Depart from me") and Jesus ("Do not be afraid").

Dan *calls to mind* (first step) the content of this Scripture: "As I read this Gospel...." He then *ponders* (second step) its meaning: "What *struck* me was....I *thought* of the spiritual boldness....I was seized by the *thought* that...I *saw* [understood] Peter as a typical man....I *understood* him as saying....It *seemed to me* that this dialogue reflects...." And Dan's heart *embraces* (third step) with love and desire the truths he has pondered: "Peter's words...really *captured* me....I was *seized* by the thought....And so I *don't want* Jesus to go." As with Thérèse, the three steps succeed one another freely in Dan's meditation.

This then is Ignatius's fundamental intuition with regard to *meditation:* as we call to mind, ponder, and embrace the truths in a Scripture passage, *God speaks* this Word to our hearts, and we are transformed. Through this threefold human capacity, our hearts can hear God speak and can reply. Such divine-human dialogue, heart to heart, is meditation.

Chapter Three

The Body of the Prayer: Contemplation

And I see clearly, and I saw afterward, that God desires that if we are going to please him and receive his great favors, we must do so through the most sacred humanity of Christ, in whom he takes his delight.

— St. Teresa of Ávila

A Threefold Process

For Ignatius, three closely related imaginative activities are involved in contemplating Scripture. As we have seen, when Mark prays with the Gospel of the Good Shepherd, the loving *reflective* approach predominates. The same is true of Thérèse's prayer with 1 Corinthians 12–13 and of Dan's prayer with the catch of fish.

When Kathryn prays with Jesus' passion, however, the *imaginative* approach predominates. She tells us that "the scene came alive in my imagination." She says, "I placed myself completely into that scene." She *sees* the *persons* in the scene: "I saw Jesus standing before Pontius Pilate and his accusers." Her heart *hears* Jesus speak *words* of self-surrender: "I began to hear Jesus saying quietly to the crowd, 'Yes. Take me. Do what you want with me, for my death will be your salvation.' "[8] She *witnesses* the *events* narrated in the Gospel: "I saw Jesus dragged off by those who wanted him dead."

35

And Kathryn *participates personally* in the events: "The moment of terror *I felt,* as his final walk through Jerusalem began, was excruciating. I prayed many hours, holding that terror in my heart, *desiring to comfort Jesus.*" "I had told Jesus I would not leave him alone, and so *I stayed there* keeping watch." Kathryn is herself an actor as these events unfold.[9]

In Ignatius's vocabulary, such imaginative participation in a Gospel event is *contemplation:* the loving *imaginative* process by which we enter God's Word and hear that Word as spoken personally to us today. In this manner of praying, Ignatius tells us, we imaginatively *see the persons* in the Gospel event, we *hear the words* they speak, and we *observe the actions* they accomplish in the event.[10] As we have just seen, this is precisely what Kathryn does when she prays with Jesus' passion — and her prayer heals her heart. We may outline this threefold imaginative process in the following way. In each successive point (in Kathryn's case, Jesus' trial, his final walk through Jerusalem, and the hours on the cross):

* I *see* the *persons*
* I *hear* the *words*
* I *observe* the *actions*

The process by which I imaginatively see the persons, hear the words, and observe the actions of a Gospel scene, participating personally in the event, is Ignatian *contemplation.* These three imaginative activities will mingle freely as I imaginatively live the Gospel event.[11]

How Do I Know It Is Not Just My Imagination?

Do I have such freedom in praying with Gospel events? Can I, like Kathryn, imaginatively enter the scene and see, hear, and observe? Can I, like her, be personally active in the scene? And can I trust that God's grace will operate in this imaginative approach? How can I know it is not "just my imagination"?

Ignatius's answer, itself rooted in the tradition that preceded him, clearly affirms our freedom to pray with the Scriptures not only reflectively (meditation) but also imaginatively (contemplation). Several observations may be made in this regard.[12]

Many saints — Ignatius himself, Teresa of Ávila, Francis de Sales, and Jane Frances de Chantal, to name a few — and countless dedicated people over the centuries have found God through imaginative contemplation. Kathryn and all who, like her, imaginatively contemplate a Gospel scene stand upon firm ground in our spiritual tradition.

Further, Scripture itself is often imaginative literature: it recounts events intended to engage our imaginations. When Kathryn says of her prayer that "I saw Jesus standing before Pontius Pilate and his accusers," that "I saw Jesus dragged off by those who wanted him dead," that "I kept the cross before my eyes" — that is, that in each case "the scene came alive in my imagination and my heart" — she is clearly reading the passion account as Scripture intends. The narrative is meant to engage not only our minds but also our imaginations.

Finally, the Scripture text itself guides the work of our imagination and so ensures the essential authenticity of such imaginative prayer. This is evident in Kathryn's prayer in which everything — all that she imaginatively sees, hears, and observes — though experienced in deeply personal ways, is solidly rooted in the Scriptures. Everything in her imaginative sharing in Jesus' passion has the ring of solid biblical truth.[13]

We trust, then, that the Spirit, who "comes to the aid of our weakness" (Rom. 8:26) when we pray, will guide not only the activity of our minds, but also the work of our imaginations. Should questions arise as we pray imaginatively, we may speak with and seek guidance from a knowledgeable person — a point to which we shall return. In our present reflections, two further examples will expand our understanding of Ignatian contemplation.

"I Took the Place of Zacchaeus"

Richard has prayed with Scripture daily for many years. He says:

> I was at Sunday Mass, and the Gospel reading was the encounter of Jesus with Zacchaeus [Luke 19:1–10]. The homily moved me when the priest spoke about Jesus' desire to be with Zacchaeus. It touched something in me, and I knew that I would pray the next day with this Gospel.
>
> When I did, I took the place of Zacchaeus. I was there in the tree, waiting for Jesus to pass by. When I imagine the Gospel, I don't see things in great detail. I just had a sense of being in the tree, waiting for Jesus to come. Then he did come, and he stopped. I sensed that, for him, at that moment, I was all that mattered. He was giving me his entire attention. And that was where the prayer stopped — Jesus looking at me, with his whole attention, with warmth, with desire to be with me, and my looking at him in response. It was quiet and happy. It lightened my worry and self-doubt. I knew that Jesus wanted to be with Zacchaeus regardless of Zacchaeus's sinfulness, and that by being with him, simply by letting him know that he was loved, Zacchaeus would be

transformed. I felt that Jesus was with me in the same way. Then I heard Jesus say, "Richard, come down quickly, for today I must stay at your house." And we were together in the house, without many words, just together.

This is clearly a blessed experience of imaginative contemplation. In his own way, without an abundance of imaginative detail, Richard sees the persons, hears the words, and observes the actions. He lives the Gospel narrative, personally present in the place of Zacchaeus. And the prayer grows warm as they meet, "Jesus looking at me ... and my looking at him in response." At this point, imaginative contemplation has reached its deep center: the healing encounter of the human heart and the divine heart.

"Let the Children Come to Me"

Anne first experienced Ignatian contemplation a year ago when she made a week of retreat. She made the retreat in the ordinary circumstances of her daily life. Each morning, before work, she would spend time in prayer. Then she would meet the retreat director in the evening and discuss her prayer. A few days into the retreat, she prayed with Jesus' encounter with children (Matt. 19:13–15). She describes the experience:

> The first times of prayer had been frustrating. Then I prayed with the passage about Jesus and the children. The retreat director had given me a list of Scripture texts. I don't know why, but I was drawn to this text and just kept reading it over and over, for about ten to fifteen minutes. It spoke of how they wanted to bring the children to Jesus, but the disciples tried to keep them from Jesus. And Jesus said, "Let them come." I

saw myself as one of the children, hugged by Jesus. It was an amazing experience. I felt so loved, so at peace. It was like when you give a child something, even a small thing, and the child gets so happy. It was just a small hug, but I felt so loved. I didn't see Jesus' face, but I could feel his beard. I was so at peace, so happy.

It was my first experience of imaginative prayer. It made me curious about this kind of prayer, and I wanted to know how to continue this.

Ever since that encounter with Jesus and experiencing that he loves me so much, I feel like I have more love to give, and I want to make others happy. Before, I would give to others if they had given to me. Now I'm more giving.

Again we stand on holy ground. Anne contemplates the Gospel scene imaginatively and participates personally in it: "I saw myself as one of the children, hugged by Jesus.... I felt so loved." This prayer not only gives joy to her heart, but also changes her life: "Ever since that encounter with Jesus ... I feel like I have more love to give, and I want to make others happy." Such growth in love confirms beyond any doubt the authenticity of this prayer.

Can I Pray This Way?

A practical question surfaces at this point: Can *I* contemplate the Gospel imaginatively like Richard and Anne do? Do I have the imaginative capacity to pray this way? What if my imagination is not like theirs? Can *I* hope to pray with this imaginative approach?

One woman speaks of her experience:

When I pray this imaginative way, it can be a little anxiety-provoking. I wonder whether anything will happen. When I reflect on the meaning of the Scripture, I have the sense that something will surface. Gospel contemplation is a bit more of a step into the unknown. It helps to read and reread the passage. This anchors it. Then there will be some little hold that allows me to enter the surface of the text and go in. It takes a bit of patience and trust. For example, the leper [Mark 1:40–45] falls on his knees. That gesture will speak to something in me, some desire. Then I just go with it and follow what opens up.

I tend to focus more on Jesus. For example, Jesus turns and looks at the crowd [Luke 14:25]. What do I feel at that point? I sense the drama of that gesture — Jesus stopping, turning toward the people, and looking at them. Then I stay with this, following where it leads my heart.

This woman too has faced these questions, wondering as she imaginatively enters the scene "whether anything will happen." She has learned that "it takes a bit of *patience* and *trust*": the patience of continuing fidelity to this prayer and trust that God truly assists our imaginative efforts. This patience and trust have led her to a personal way of imaginatively contemplating Gospel scenes; she has learned to recognize that point of entry, that "little hold that allows me to enter the surface of the text and go in."

Another woman recalls:

When I first started imagining the Gospel, it was really difficult. I listened to the ones teaching us and I thought: Are they crazy? Why should I put myself there in the Gospel? It was really hard.

The first thing I was able to feel imaginatively was the weather. I could feel the heat in Jerusalem, for example. They suggested that we imagine with all of our senses. I couldn't imagine with the sense of smell. As I continued to pray this way, my ability to do it grew. Now if I'm praying with a Gospel scene by the sea, for example, I can hear the sea, I can feel the wind. I still can't use my sense of smell. I can feel and I can see.

I was praying with Jesus walking on the water [Matt. 14:22–33] at the point where Jesus says to Peter, "Come." I could see what was happening. I could feel the cold and the wind. I was one of those in the boat, sitting there as one of the passengers. I could see that Peter was really scared, and I thought of times when I've been afraid too, wondering what was going to happen to me. And, like Peter, I started shouting out to Jesus too, to save us.

This woman too is finding her way in imaginative contemplation. She notes how difficult it was at first. As she perseveres in contemplation, her ease with this method grows, and now she can hear and feel the Gospel scene. She has also discovered which of her imaginative senses assist her more and which less, at this point, in such contemplation. She prays according to her personal imaginative strengths.

A man says of his prayer with Scripture:

When the Scripture passage is visual, I try to *see* what's happening. I stand outside the events and see. And I hear the words. I make the words of Christ words *to me,* so that it becomes more like a dialogue. When Christ speaks, I put my name before the words: "Michael, I am the bread of life," "Michael, without me you can do nothing." This makes it very concrete and personal. It's not just Jesus talking to the disciples, but to me. The words become much more engrained this way.

Sometimes I ask the Lord questions: Why do you talk to the [Syrophoenician] woman this way when she asks help for her daughter [Mark 7:24–30]? The answer comes, like a light — something you never thought about. It hits you at the center. It brings up issues in my life. They are there, but I never faced them. I strongly believe that it is the Lord who brings them to the fore.

Sometimes I become the person. I *am* the Syrophoenician woman, and I explain the whole story to a third person. I take her position; I let her tell the story to the Lord or to a third person. I speak based on what I think she is going through. As I do this, it's going to touch my story. For example, the woman says, "You didn't do what I asked you." For me, this becomes: Is there something that I asked for, over and over, and you didn't do? Am I angry about this?

Sometimes I get images, sometimes not. If I don't, then I take the part of the person and do this kind of dialogue.

This man too has found his personal imaginative way: "I make the words of Christ words to me, so that it becomes more like a dialogue"; "Sometimes I ask the Lord questions"; "Sometimes I become the person...and I explain the whole story to a third person." We sense that this man, after faithful practice of imaginative contemplation, is at home in such prayer and finds great blessing in it: "The answer comes, like a light.... It hits you at the center.... It's going to touch my story."

The individual ways of contemplating are endlessly varied. Each person's experience will be a *personal* approach to the general method. Those who use this method will find their own ways of contemplating, in accordance with their own ways of imagining.[14] As is evident in the accounts quoted, ease in imaginative prayer normally grows through faithful practice over time. The experience of such prayer will guide us to our own way of contemplating. Once again, if questions surface as we pray, conversation with a knowledgeable person will greatly assist us.

The Body of the Prayer: Meditation and Contemplation

Thus far we have focused on *the body of the prayer* in meditation and contemplation. The greater part of our time in meditation or contemplation will generally be occupied in this: calling to mind the truths in the passage, pondering them, and embracing them (*meditation*); or seeing the persons, hearing the words, and observing the actions in the scene (*contemplation*).

At the heart of these methods lies a simple intuition: that we may enter the Word of God both *reflectively* and *imaginatively*. These methods are simply gateways, open doors into the richness of God's Word. In fact, Ignatius never attempts to specify what will happen once we have passed that door. Having entered reflectively or imaginatively, our hearts are utterly free to follow the drawings of grace: as Kathryn stays by Jesus on the cross; as Mark lets the words of the Good Shepherd text "swim" and reverberate in his heart; as Richard simply gazes at Jesus, who gazes at him; as Anne receives the love expressed in Jesus' hug; as a woman is drawn by the gesture of Jesus who turns and faces the crowd . . . and so forth, in the endlessly creative freedom of the Spirit.

Which method will we choose? In part, the choice will depend upon our personal inclinations and the promptings of grace in the moment. (Mark is drawn to pray imaginatively with the catch of fish and says, "I was *in* the story"; Dan is drawn to pray reflectively with the same text and ponders the meaning of Peter's words, "Depart from me.") In part, it will depend upon the Scripture passage itself: texts that recount events (the passion, the catch of fish, Jesus' encounter with children) offer themselves more readily to contemplation than those that state truths without narrative (the Good Shepherd knows his own, love is the heart of our vocation in the Church).

At times, elements of both methods will mingle in a single time of prayer.[15] Steve describes his prayer with the parable of the Pharisee and the tax collector (Luke 18:9–14), and says:

> I read in the first verse that Jesus told this parable to "those who were convinced of their own righteousness and despised everyone else." I asked myself: who are the others whom I judge? I don't despise others, but I may judge others somewhat negatively. Am I bitter toward anyone? Do I hold anyone not in a good light? Out of this came the insight that there are some whom I've judged, and I decided that I would pray for them.
>
> I entered the scene and stood there as the Pharisee. I saw him standing off by himself and asked myself when I am not in community. I heard what he was saying. I looked at my own life to see where I might just be satisfied with myself, where I might not be allowing God's love to help me be honest. That's been my prayer this week. And there are some things about which I think of myself in good terms. I felt a sense of gratitude to God for these gifts. I know that they are his gifts, from my family and my experiences in life.
>
> Then I took the place of the tax collector, who wouldn't even look up to heaven. He saw his weak side.

I allowed my weaknesses to be exposed to God, not really trying to solve them or eliminate them, but just allowing them to be open to God. As a result I've felt called this week to look at my own need for humility.

A richness of blessings arises in Steve as he prays: gratitude for God's gifts, desire for honesty before God, review of his relationships, prayer for others, a renewed search for humility. At times, Steve prays in a more *meditative* mode, as when he reflects on the meaning of the first verse. At this point the *reflective* approach clearly predominates. At other times, Steve prays in a more *contemplative* mode, as when he enters the scene and takes the place, first of the Pharisee, then of the tax collector, hearing their words and observing their gestures. At this point the *imaginative* approach is clearly primary.

When Kathryn prays with Jesus' passion, her prayer is essentially contemplative. When Mark prays with the Gospel of the Good Shepherd, his prayer is essentially meditative. When Steve prays, he freely combines elements of both methods. Such freedom is always ours in prayer. And, as these experiences indicate, such freedom is fruitful in the Lord.

Chapter Four

Before the Prayer Begins

How I wish he would enkindle me with that fire of divine love. The flames of his love burn beyond the stars; may the longing for his overwhelming delights and the divine fire ever burn within me!

— St. Columban

"My Heart Is Ready, O God"

At this point we have seen the essential intuition that underlies meditation and contemplation: the human capacity to enter the Word of God reflectively and imaginatively, with great freedom then to follow the promptings of the Spirit in the prayer. *Everything else* Ignatius will say about these methods is in service of this essential intuition — that is, of the body of the prayer — whether as preparation for it, or as means to conserve its fruit.

These further counsels matter. The fruitfulness of the body of the prayer depends to a large degree upon what precedes and what follows it. In this chapter we will explore the choices that *precede* the prayer: what these choices are, why they matter, and how they may be fruitfully made. We will begin by listening as five persons of faithful prayer describe their own choices in preparing for prayer. We will then examine what these experiences teach us and how Ignatius's counsels may assist us in preparing to pray.

47

"I Always Take Something from the Gospels"

Charles began praying with Scripture eight months ago. He says:

> I try to pray with Scripture as often as I can. I do it when I find time for it, usually about once every two days. I pray before the Blessed Sacrament if I can, for about forty-five minutes. If I pray at home, I do it before going to bed. I have found that nighttime works best for me when I pray at home. During the day my mind is filled with thoughts of work.
>
> I choose a Scripture by opening the Bible and flipping through it. I always take something from the Gospels. I'm still new at this. I haven't done it a lot, and the Gospels are the texts I can pray with best. I look for something where there is an activity, a movement — for example, the feeding of the five thousand [Matt. 14:13–21], the calming of the storm [Matt. 8:23–27], or the call of the Twelve [Mark 3:13–19]. I look until I feel satisfied that this is the one God wants. It might be one that relates to some struggle in the day. Then I begin the prayer.

Charles makes several choices in preparation for prayer. He chooses a *place* and a *time* that work best for him, adapting these flexibly according to his day at work. He then chooses a *Scripture* suited to his spiritual needs, "the one God wants" for him that day. He identifies this passage by looking through the Gospels until he finds a text "where there is an activity" (an event) which speaks to his present experience. Then Charles is ready to begin his contemplation.

"It Has to Be Something That Moves Me"

Carol learned to pray with Scripture when she made an Ignatian retreat some years ago. She says:

> I usually pray in the evening. I can't in the morning because of family needs, but often I am more free in the evening. I shut the door, and I have a quiet space. I have a book on the Spiritual Exercises that I like, and often I find my Scripture there. Sometimes I take the Gospel reading of the coming Sunday. Whether it's one way or the other, it has to be something that moves me. If nothing does, then I pull out the *Spiritual Exercises*. I look through the Scriptures there [*SpirEx*, 261–312] and choose one.

Carol too, in the circumstances of her family life, chooses the time and place that best help her to pray. She has developed her own way of choosing a Scripture for prayer, drawing upon three sources: a book on the Spiritual Exercises which gives Scriptures for prayer, the Gospel of the coming Sunday, and the Scriptures given in the *Spiritual Exercises* themselves. She is attentive, above all, to choose a Scripture that speaks to her *personally*: "It has to be something that moves me." We readily perceive how such preparation will bless Carol's prayer once she begins.

"I've Gone Systematically through the Gospels"

Robert began praying with Scripture six years ago. He describes how he prepares for prayer:

> Over these years I've gone systematically through the Gospels, one by one. The evening before, I read the Gospel I'm going through until a passage strikes me. I don't necessarily pray with the one which follows the

last one I prayed with. I pray with the next one that strikes me.

Sometimes I choose a text based on what I'm experiencing that day. Or it might be from something that strikes me in spiritual reading I've done that day. For example, one time I was reading about the Holy Eucharist. So I prayed with John 6 [the discourse on the bread of life] and with the Last Supper [the institution of the Eucharist]. I stay with these texts as long as I find fruit. Sometimes I repeat a passage if it speaks to me. Another time I was reading a book on union with Christ. The author mentioned John 14–16 and spoke about the Mystical Body of Christ. So I spent two weeks praying with those chapters in John's Gospel. I went over them two or three times, and I felt them more deeply each time. When things strike me like this, I set aside the systematic prayer with the Gospels, and I pick it up again when I've finished.

I go through the Gospels in order: Matthew, Mark, Luke, and John. When I've finished, I start again. The first two years I jumped around quite a lot. Then I began this systematic way. Now I've been through the Gospels two or three times.

I prepare for the prayer the evening before. I choose the Scripture and then I read a short commentary on it, not a heavy intellectual one. I read the Gospel passage two or three times before going to bed. I do my prayer the next morning at the start of the day.

Robert, after some initial searching — "The first two years I jumped around quite a lot" — has found a flexible approach to prayer that serves him well. His systematic prayer with the four Gospels ensures that he is never without solid material for prayer. At the same time, his freedom to choose personally within the Gospels and to follow other leadings as they arise, ensures that the text chosen will speak personally to him. His heart sets the pace for his progress through the Gospels: "I stay with these texts as long as I find fruit."

For Robert, the beginning of the day is the best time for prayer. He prepares the evening before by choosing his text, reading it two or three times, and reviewing a brief spiritual commentary on the text. Clearly, his heart will be ready when morning and his time of prayer arrive the following day.

"Generally I Use the Daily Readings for Mass"

Monica has been praying with Scripture for many years. She comments:

> I follow the Lectionary [book with the readings for Mass] in choosing my Scripture for daily prayer. Every so often I may use a different passage if one suggests itself, but generally I use the daily readings for Mass. This helps me feel more engaged with the Church.
>
> It's not always easy for me to find a place to pray. I work three nights a week, and it's often hard to get up even in time to help the children. I can't get a consistent time for prayer in the morning. So I look at my agenda and set a time. I can look ahead and set a time for the next day. Sometimes when I take the children to soccer practice or karate, I can sit for forty-five minutes and do it. But I tend to need a more quiet space. I do it at home when the children are at school. When I can, I do it for about fifty minutes.

Monica has found her own source of Scripture for daily prayer: the readings from the Mass of the day. This offers her a selection of Scriptures (first reading, psalm, Gospel) for prayer each day without fail. Her choice also links her personal prayer with the liturgical seasons and with the Church at prayer: "This helps me feel more engaged with the Church." Monica too, like the others, follows her "system" with some freedom and flexibility. Because her schedule changes daily, Monica plans ahead and chooses the best time and place for each day's prayer.

"I Pray with the Sunday Gospel throughout the Week"

A final witness provides yet another approach to prayer. Brian, too, has prayed with Scripture for many years, and says:

> I pray with the Sunday Gospel throughout the week. I spend my prayer time on Friday and Saturday preparing this Gospel. I read the Gospel, and then the passages which precede and follow it. That helps me to understand this particular Gospel better. I look at which evangelist [Matthew, Mark, Luke, or John] wrote this Gospel passage. That too helps me to understand it better. Then I look at a Bible that has wonderful study notes, and I read the notes for this Gospel. Finally, I look at a commentary — though, by this time I may already be reflecting on the text. On Sunday I hear the Gospel proclaimed and the homily, and that too becomes part of my preparation.
>
> Then, from Sunday through Thursday, I pray on this Gospel. I need that many days to pray with it. I'm usually not finished with it after I pray. When I come back to the same Gospel I'm reminded of the readings I've done about it, or I may sit with another part of it. Things that happen during the week come into the prayer.
>
> My best time for prayer is in the afternoon or evening, when the others are out and the house is quiet. I'm at

my best in the evening. I have a comfortable chair in my room — I call it my "God chair." I have a table there with a candle, my Bible, and the other readings I've done. I usually pray for about a half hour.

The link between Brian's personal prayer and that of the Church is evident: the Sunday Gospel is the heart of his entire week of prayer. The choice of a single Gospel for the week's prayer permits Brian to enter it deeply, returning to it day after day. His dedicated effort to understand the text is noteworthy. Brian's attentive reading of various sources — the text itself, study notes, a commentary — opens for him the meaning of the Gospel and nourishes his prayer.

Preparing for Prayer

Various choices, then, must be made if our prayer with Scripture is to be fruitful. Like these persons, we must choose the *time* — how long, and at what point in the day — we can give to this prayer. Like them, we must choose a *place:* in the presence of the Eucharist in church, or seated in my "God chair" in the silence of my room, or in the quietest place available while the children are at soccer practice — whatever setting best helps us to pray.[16] One high school teacher told me that each morning she arrives in her classroom twenty minutes before her students and there prays with Scripture. This is the one place of quiet she can find, and she loves the prayerful quality with which her teaching day begins. Another, whose living conditions rarely offer a space of quiet, downloads a guided reflection on a Scripture for the day and prayerfully listens to it during her thirty-minute subway ride to work each day. Such creativity in the Spirit opens the way to great blessings.

Again, like these persons, we must choose a *Scripture* for prayer. All of these have found a personal *structure* to which they adhere *flexibly:* prayer with the successive Gospels, with the daily readings for Mass, with the Sunday Gospel, and so forth — always with the freedom to dwell with a Scripture that speaks to their hearts, or to pray with other texts that may draw them that day. This wise combination of structure and flexibility renders such prayer fruitful and sustainable.

These persons speak of preparing for prayer with the aid of a *commentary* of some kind: a book that presents Scriptures according to the Spiritual Exercises, a Bible with notes, a brief spiritual commentary, a reflection downloaded from the Internet. In various ways, they prepare before the actual time of the prayer. In the *Spiritual Exercises,* Ignatius suggests that this be done briefly *the evening before,* that this Scripture be our final thought upon retiring, and that we gently dwell on this Scripture as we begin the following day.[17] This practice allows the Scripture to germinate in our hearts, in a certain sense, as the prayer approaches. A heart so prepared is truly "ready" to encounter God (Ps. 57:7).

Such wise and creative choices bring us to the threshold of the prayer itself. In our next chapter we will examine Ignatius's counsels for crossing this threshold.

Chapter Five

Beginning the Prayer

I leave you my faith in the presence of God, of the God who is all Love dwelling in our souls. I confide to you: it is this intimacy with Him "within" which has been the beautiful sun illuminating my life.
— Blessed Elizabeth of the Trinity

When Heart Speaks to Heart

When we meet a close friend and begin to speak, the conversation generally does not begin at the deep point. Most often we greet each other, settle ourselves physically, and speak for some minutes about whatever comes to mind: how the day has gone, how we have been since we last spoke, or any other matters of the moment. Eventually the conversation may reach the deep point in which heart speaks profoundly to heart. The initial minutes do not yet contain that deep sharing. Without them, however, we would seldom reach that deep communication for which our hearts long.

The same is true of communication with God in prayer. We generally do not begin our prayer at the deep point of communion with God. Most often, as we begin, we need time simply to enter the prayer: to disengage from other concerns and to awaken the "inmost inwardness" of our hearts where, in faith, we encounter the God we love.[18]

Certainly, God's grace is sovereign and may engage us at any point in prayer — even in its very beginning. Similarly, when friends meet they may, on occasion, enter almost immediately into profound sharing. Such immediacy, however, is to be received as a gift. We cannot *presume* that this will be the case. More often, our hearts will need these initial minutes to enter gently into prayer. Many struggles in prayer cease when this natural need of the heart is respected.

Ignatius, ever attuned to the human heart, offers wise counsel regarding these initial minutes in prayer. In so doing, he is simply articulating what our hearts, at their best, already know. When we begin prayer, we want to be *aware of the Lord* who is with us. We want to be *available* to God. We want to be *alive to the content of the Word of God*. We want to be *engaged in that Word*. And we want to pray in *humble dependence on God's grace*. These are the dispositions Ignatius highlights in his teaching on meditation and contemplation. As always, he offers simple and effective means by which we may pursue them.

Charles is now seated before the Blessed Sacrament in church, ready to begin his prayer with the Gospel. Carol has shut the door to her room in the evening quiet, and is about to pray with Scripture. Robert has risen in the early morning and now is settled in his place of prayer with Scripture. Monica's children are at school, and the house is quiet as she prepares to pray with God's Word. Brian is now seated in his "God chair," Bible at hand, ready to begin his prayer.

How should these persons employ the first minutes of their prayer? What will help them enter that deep space in which heart speaks to heart?

In this chapter we will review Ignatius's counsels for these first minutes of prayer.[19] As in past chapters, we will discuss each in the light of concrete experience.

"I Will Consider How God Our Lord Looks upon Me"

Barbara began to pray with Scripture several months ago. She describes her practice:

> I pray in the evening in my apartment. This is when I most easily find a quiet space. I have a cup of tea, and begin. I usually spend about fifteen minutes in the prayer.
>
> I turn the television and the radio off. I begin by making sure I am at peace. I try to picture God talking to me, or just with me. I take a few deep breaths and settle down. I let my mind be empty and open. Then I open the Scripture and read it.

Barbara is conscious of the importance of these initial minutes in prayer. She ensures a space of quiet for her prayer: "I turn the television and the radio off." She readies herself physically and emotionally: "I take a few deep breaths and settle down." And these initial minutes are *relational*: "I try to picture *God talking to me,* or just *with me.*" From the outset, Barbara consciously calls to mind God's presence with her as she prays. Her prayer is *being with* the God who *speaks personally* to her. The "picturing" involved is a human means of expressing a profound truth of faith.

Richard says of his prayer:

> I usually pray in the morning after I rise. For me this is the best time. I rise, prepare, have a cup of coffee, and begin my prayer. I begin by standing for a few minutes and thinking of each Person of the Trinity. I think of the Father as close to me, and as saying, "You are my beloved son" [see Matt. 3:17]. Then I imagine Jesus standing at my side, and I think of these words: "Jesus, looking at him, loved him" [Mark 10:21]. I feel that

look of love. Then I think of the Holy Spirit dwelling in my heart as Love, Gift, Spiritual Anointing, or some other title of the Holy Spirit. Sometimes I feel the presence of these divine Persons more than others, but this always helps me know that I am in the Trinity's presence as I pray, and to know that I am loved. Then I do as St. Ignatius says and express this awareness through a bow or a moment of kneeling. Then I sit. I call to mind the content of my prayer, and then I begin.

For Richard, as for Barbara, these initial minutes are deeply relational. Richard begins his prayer by consciously calling to mind the presence of the three divine Persons. He senses the love for him in the Trinity, and his prayer begins with a lively consciousness of that love. Richard expresses this consciousness even physically, "through a bow or a moment of kneeling." We sense that these few minutes lead Richard to a point of great readiness for prayer: "Then I sit. I call to mind the content of my prayer, and then I begin."

One who watched Ignatius pray on the terrace of the community's house in Rome describes how Ignatius himself began his prayer:

> He would stand there and take off his hat; without stirring he would fix his eyes on the heavens for a short while. Then, sinking to his knees, he would make a lowly gesture of reverence to God. After that he would sit on a bench, for his body's weakness did not permit him to do otherwise. There he was, head uncovered, tears trickling drop by drop, in such sweetness and silence, that no sob, no sigh, no noise, no movement of the body was noticed.[20]

Again we stand on holy ground. As Ignatius's prayer begins, the witness tells us, "he would stand there" fixing his eyes on the heavens, profoundly aware of God's presence. Then, "sinking to his knees, he would make a lowly gesture of reverence to God" and so enter into prayer. Ignatius's prayer begins immediately as relationship with the God who loves him.

Ignatius counsels us to begin our prayer in a similar way. He writes:

> A step or two before the place where I am to contemplate or meditate, I will stand for the space of an Our Father, with my understanding raised on high, considering how God our Lord looks upon me, etc., and I will make a gesture of reverence or humility. (*SpirEx*, 75)[21]

We begin our prayer by *considering how God our Lord looks upon us:* the love in the divine gaze upon us. This moment is brief — "for the space of an Our Father" — but is of the greatest importance for prayer. Through it, our prayer immediately becomes what it most profoundly is — *relationship:* the human person in relationship with God.

Barbara and Richard, like Ignatius himself, have found their personal ways of considering the love with which God looks upon them as they begin their prayer. What will our ways be? The search for these ways will richly bless our prayer.[22]

I Offer All My Will and Actions to God (Preparatory Prayer)

Ignatius now invites us to ask for *availability* to God in the prayer that lies ahead. He calls this the "preparatory prayer" and writes: "The preparatory prayer is to ask grace of God our Lord, that all my intentions, actions, and operations be purely ordered in the service and praise of his divine

majesty" (*SpirEx,* 46).[23] Those who pray will find personal
expressions of this prayer for availability.

Monica describes her experience of this preparatory
prayer:

> When I made the Spiritual Exercises in daily life,[24] my
> director asked me to write my own preparatory prayer.
> Since I said that prayer daily for several months, I
> learned it by heart. I put it on a card which I still
> have. My preparatory prayer is this: "In this prepara-
> tory prayer, I will ask the Lord to hold me fast, to show
> me clearly that all is grace and that everything in my life
> speaks of God's love, to direct my thoughts, words, and
> actions to the praise and service of God alone, so that
> I might grow in joy and gratitude in God's kingdom of
> compassionate care."
>
> I say this prayer every time I begin to pray with Scrip-
> ture. For me, an experience hangs on every one of these
> words. They are like a collection of stopped time. I ask
> the Lord "to hold me fast." For me these words have a
> sense of being in my spiritual home. For a long time I
> felt kind of homeless. This kind of prayer is a time and
> place where I am held fast and feel secure in a way. I
> wrote the word "clearly" in the phrase "to show me
> clearly that all is grace" because I remember picking
> up a prayer card when I was in my twenties that used
> that word as in "to know God's will for me clearly." I
> added that word very specifically since I am often seek-
> ing clarity in discernment. This prayer also speaks to
> my deepest desire: to be mindful that all is grace, to
> live in joy and gratitude, in God's kingdom of compas-
> sion and care. There is something concrete for me in
> this. I can understand how to participate in this. I can

see his kingdom in compassionate care, my own and that of others.

How will we make this prayer for availability? Will we use Ignatius's words? Will we, like Monica, find our own? Will we pray it in the same words each time? Will we express it in varied ways? What will happen in our prayer if, like Monica, we ask for availability to God each time we begin?

I Review the Scripture for This Prayer

Ignatius then invites us to review the Scripture for prayer. This brief review renders the text fully present to us on the threshold of our prayer with it.[25]

Mark notes:

> When I am ready to pray, I ask for grace. I ask the Trinity, the Holy Spirit, to descend upon me and enlighten me. Then I read the Scripture three or four times. Then I may pray a bit to Jesus to ask him something, or just to say, "I love you." Then, after I've read it three or four times, I close my eyes and can focus in the scene, letting myself go in the Spirit.

Here Mark, in his own way, does exactly what Ignatius suggests. As his prayer is about to begin, he reviews the text, rendering its content fresh in his mind and heart. Then, he says, "I close my eyes and can focus in the scene, *letting myself go in the Spirit.*" Mark's words express the purpose of this brief review: because the Scripture is now alive in our consciousness, we are *set free* to enter that Scripture.

Elizabeth says of her prayer:

> I would get up early, before work, to pray. I would get settled in my chair. I would begin my prayer by talking to God very informally, just saying, "Jesus, here I am."

I would make a little prayer to get rid of the cares of the day. I would have a note pad with me so that if things came up I could write them down, and they wouldn't be a distraction to me. I would calm myself and read the Scripture two or three times. Then I would be still, and the prayer would come.

Like Mark, Elizabeth also reviews the Scripture as she begins. And, like Mark, she is set free to pray: "Then I would be still, and the prayer would come." As we begin, such a review may bless our prayer as well.

I Imaginatively Enter the Place of This Scripture (Composition)

With the content of the Scripture now present to us, Ignatius invites us to *engage ourselves imaginatively* in the text. He speaks of this as "composition, seeing the place" (*SpirEx*, 112). He invites us, that is, to "compose" ourselves imaginatively within the event described in the text. This composition, Ignatius says, "will be to see with the sight of the imagination the material place where the thing I wish to contemplate is found" (*SpirEx*, 47). Through this brief imaginative act, I enter the place of the Scripture — *I am there*, engaged in its content.

The following is a description of St. Jane Frances de Chantal's prayer with Scripture:

Jane Frances, when she was a widow caring for her little children, would read a Gospel passage carefully. Next, she would picture the scene with elaborate care, noting Christ, the disciples, the crowd, the centurion in the foreground [Matt. 8:5–13], and would then listen to his act of faith. She would study his expression and the reactions of the crowd, ponder his words and their meaning in the imaginative setting that she had composed. Here was her backcloth. Weeks later, she had only to recall the scene and say, "Lord, I am not worthy," and the content of the centurion's prayer flooded back. Later she found that she had only to say the one word "Lord," and she could pray as he had; finally, she said no words but allowed the scene to calm her until she became the centurion.[26]

After Jane Frances had read the Scripture, she "would picture the scene." This setting formed a backdrop for her prayer, a place from which she could enter the profound meaning of the event. Clearly, this imaginative setting engages her deeply in the Scripture and assists her to assimilate its meaning.

Brian says of his prayer:

When I pray with a Gospel event, I enter the scene by trying to look at the surroundings. I ask myself: What does this place look like? Where am I in that setting? Am I sitting? Standing? I focus on Jesus. What is he like? Is there tension in the air? Peace? What kind of day is it? Are there people around? Are we in a desert place? In a town? What is life like in this place? Are there conversations going on? And where am I in relationship to Jesus? Who am I in this event? Often I like to be an observer, among the disciples. Sometimes I take a role: I might be the blind man, or a Pharisee.

Brian, too, imaginatively "composes" himself in the Scripture: "When I pray with a Gospel event *I enter the scene* by trying *to look at the surroundings*." As with Jane Frances, this brief imaginative act engages Brian in the event he is about to contemplate.

Even when the prayer is meditative (reflection on truths), this imaginative composition may be of assistance.[27] Persons who meditate, for example, on the Beatitudes (Matt. 5:3–12) may find the setting described — the mountain, the crowd, the disciples at Jesus' feet — of great value for their meditation. To "compose" themselves in this imaginative setting may provide a blessed backdrop for their prayerful reflection on the successive Beatitudes.

Kevin notes:

> When I begin my prayer, I generally see Jesus as seated before me, just a few feet away, the way friends sit facing each other as they speak. It helps me be aware that he is with me as I pray. I can return to this during my prayer, and it renews my awareness of Jesus with me.

Again we stand on holy ground. Kevin, too, in his own way, has found an imaginative setting for his prayer. Clearly, a setting of this kind can assist him in meditative prayer. He will ponder Jesus' words with lively awareness of Jesus' presence to him, speaking these words to him personally.

Might Ignatius's counsel assist us as well? Might a brief imaginative "composition" help us pray more fruitfully with Scripture?

I Ask of God What I Wish and Desire in This Prayer

The final space of preparation is simply the heart. As I enter my prayer, Ignatius invites me to ask God for "what I wish and desire" in this prayer (*SpirEx*, 48). Why am I praying today? What does my heart seek? As I begin my prayer, I express my heart's desire to God and ask for its fulfillment.

Mark says: "When I'm ready to pray, I ask for grace. I ask the Trinity, the Holy Spirit, to descend upon me and enlighten me." Kathleen says:

> When I begin my prayer I always ask for the grace I asked for so often in the Spiritual Exercises — for interior knowledge of Jesus, to better praise and serve him [*SpirEx,* 104]. That's what I remember from the Exercises, and it's what I want — a relationship with Jesus.

Robert observes:

> When I begin my contemplation, I pray for help. I invoke the Lord, asking that this be for his greater glory, for my greater good, and for the good of others. First I turn to Jesus and ask him to help me see what his word for me today is. I make an act of faith, hope, and love. I ask the Holy Spirit for light. Then I read the passage.

Monica says:

> After I make my preparatory prayer, I ask for a grace. For a long time I would forget to do this. I didn't consider it important. But there is something in this, in saying, "I ask for the grace to...." Sometimes I don't know until I begin the prayer what the grace will be. It could be something from my [prayer of] examen the evening before, if something stood out. Or if I'm feeling really uplifted or really burdened, I bring this to the prayer and from this comes the grace I ask for. This almost seems to be the most important thing I do before I enter the prayer.

These persons begin their prayer, as Ignatius suggests, by asking of God what they "wish and desire" in their prayer. The desire may arise from something in the Scripture. As

I prepare to contemplate a healing in the Gospels, for example, I may ask the Lord for healing in my life. It may arise, as with Monica, from something I carry in my heart today. It may simply be, as with Robert, a request for help in the prayer I am beginning. In accord with the stirrings of my heart, I ask God for "what I wish and desire" as I begin my prayer this day.

How Do I Use These Spiritual Tools?

These, then, are the spiritual tools Ignatius offers us as we begin our prayer: to "consider how God our Lord looks upon me"; to ask for availability to God in this prayer; to review the Scripture; to engage myself imaginatively in the Scripture; and to ask for what I wish and desire in this prayer. How should we use these tools? Must we use all of them every time we pray? Must we use them in sequence? What if I am particularly drawn to one of them? What if my heart is already engaged in the Scripture as I begin?

The answers to these questions depend upon a fundamental fact — that the purpose of these tools is to *prepare* us for the body of the prayer.[28] Once our hearts are ready, the tools have served their purpose. They are a launching pad, not a straitjacket.

We may use them in sequence as Ignatius gives them. There is wisdom in doing so, since each step is itself prepared by the preceding steps. We may find it helpful to pray them this way for some time, perhaps even at length. In this way, we will learn them well. Once assimilated, these steps will be at our disposal whenever we need them. As indicated earlier, they ease many struggles in settling into prayer.

If one of these steps leads us into prayer, then, on this particular day, we may need no further steps. Whenever heart begins to speak to heart, the preparatory phase is done.

Should we find ourselves distracted in the body of the prayer, we may return briefly to one or more of these steps. Barbara begins her prayer by trying "to picture God talking to me, or just with me." In time of distraction, she may do so again, and then, engaged once more in prayer, return to the Scripture. Richard begins by seeing Jesus and considering the words, "Jesus, looking at him, loved him." In time of distraction, he may again see Jesus, feel the love in Jesus' gaze upon him, and so, engaged once more in prayer, return to the Scripture. Brian begins his prayer "by trying to look at the surroundings" in the Gospel scene (composition). In time of distraction, he may again "compose" himself imaginatively in the scene, and so, engaged once more in the prayer, return to the Scripture. The same may be said of the other steps (preparatory prayer, review of the Scripture passage, asking for what I desire) as well.

Ignatius, who knows the human heart so deeply, has supplied us with effective steps for beginning our prayer. A wise use of them will faithfully guide us toward what we "wish and desire": that happy encounter with God in which heart speaks to heart.

Chapter Six

Ending the Prayer

For me, prayer is a surge of the heart, it is a simple look turned toward heaven, it is a cry of gratitude both in time of trial and in time of joy; it is something great, something supernatural, which opens my heart and unites me with Jesus. — St. Thérèse of Lisieux

The Rhythms of the Heart

As we have seen, our hearts normally require some minutes to *prepare* for deep sharing. Similarly, they generally require some minutes to *conclude* such sharing, before they resume their habitual activity.

In conversation, friends, in their final minutes together, may communicate remaining concerns. They will express, in their individual ways, gratitude for the sharing. And after they part, they do not forget this sharing. Their hearts remain warm with the gift received, and their thoughts return to it as activity permits.

Something similar is true of prayer. When the needs of the heart are respected, deep communication with God does not end abruptly. A transitional space is necessary for the prayer to conclude gently, and for its blessing to be preserved in subsequent activity.

Ignatius is alive to this need of the heart. In this chapter we will explore his counsels regarding the conclusion of our formal time of prayer. Wisdom in applying these counsels will do much to conserve and increase the fruitfulness of our prayer.

I Speak to God as My Heart Is Moved (Colloquy)

Ignatius invites us to dedicate the final minutes of prayer to *conversation* with God. Our reflective (meditative) or imaginative (contemplative) activity in the prayer does not continue to the very end of the prayer. Ignatius invites us, as the final minutes approach, to turn from this activity to conversation — to speaking freely with God. This conversation is the "colloquy" with which the prayer normally concludes.[29]

This colloquy, Ignatius says, "is properly made by *speaking,* as one friend speaks to another, or as a servant speaks to his master; now asking for some grace, now blaming oneself for some misdeed, now communicating one's affairs, and seeking counsel in them" (*SpirEx,* 54). In the colloquy, the heart *speaks* — it communicates freely with God, according to the stirrings it feels.

When our hearts truly engage the Scriptures (God's Word to us), such colloquies (our word to God in response) arise naturally. When, for example, Thérèse meditates on 1 Corinthians 12–13, this Word of God speaks deeply to her heart: "Charity gave me the key of my vocation.... I *understood* that the Church had a Heart.... I *understood* that it was Love alone that made the Church's members act.... I *understood* that Love comprised all vocations."

Now Thérèse ceases to reflect, and her heart spontaneously *speaks to God* in reply: "Then, in the excess of my delirious joy, I cried out: O *Jesus,* my Love... my vocation, at last I have found it.... Yes, I have found my place in the Church and *it is You, O my God,* who have given me this place.... O luminous Beacon of love, *I know how to reach you,* I have found the secret of possessing your flame." When the human heart turns from reflecting or imagining in prayer, to speaking directly with God, it has entered the rich space of colloquy.

A man is meditating on the first beatitude, "Blessed are the poor in spirit, for theirs is the kingdom of heaven" (Matt. 5:3). As he reflects on the words "poor in spirit," love for Gospel simplicity awakens in his heart, and he *speaks* to Jesus, asking for this grace. A woman is contemplating the calming of the storm at sea (Matt. 8:23–7). As she imagines the scene, seeing the boat close to sinking and hearing the cry of the disciples, her heart is moved, and she *speaks* to Jesus, asking him to calm the storms in her life. This man and this woman have moved from reflecting and imagining to speaking directly to God — that is, to a colloquy.

Colloquies may arise at any time in our prayer. When they do, our prayer has reached its deepest center. Then all anxiety to move forward, all further reflecting or imagining, may be simply relinquished. This heart-to-heart communication has primacy over all else in prayer. When the colloquy has concluded, we may gently resume the reflecting or imagining.

While colloquies may arise at any time in prayer, Ignatius specifically invites us to include a colloquy at the conclusion of our prayer. Monica states:

> The colloquy helps me finish the prayer. It's a place where I talk to Jesus, to Mary, to God, about what happened in my experience of prayer. Often it's a kind of speaking that is not verbal. I spend about five to ten minutes in the colloquy. It is a "layer" that seems to complete the prayer for me. It's almost like a prism. I see all of my prayer in a different light. Something in Mary's experience speaks to mine, as, for example,

when she runs to Elizabeth (Luke 1:39). It's like a parenting moment in my own life. Or something in Jesus' story comes into contact with mine, and I speak about this with him.

Again we stand on holy ground. Monica's experience illustrates the wisdom of Ignatius's counsel: "The colloquy *helps me finish* the prayer.... It is a 'layer' that *seems to complete* the prayer for me.... I see all of my prayer in a different light." Her experience also reflects Ignatius's freedom in these colloquies. We may speak to the Trinity, or to any Person of the Trinity — Father, Son, or Holy Spirit. We may also wish, in the communion of saints, to speak with Mary or with another of the saints.[30]

Robert relates his own experience of colloquy:

I end my prayer with a colloquy. I have a system I follow. I thank God; then I ask for what I need and offer any resolutions I may have made in the prayer. I don't force them. If they come, I offer them to God. If not, I may renew old resolutions. I say "thank you" for this time of grace, of insight. I ask for graces I need in a specific way — as, for example, in my relationship with this person. So it's really three things: thanksgiving, offering of resolutions, and petition for the grace I need. I may ask these of Jesus, of the Holy Spirit, or of the Father. I also ask them of Mary.

The colloquy is where it's hard to put on a mask. It's a time for honesty about what I want, how I feel, why it's difficult to love. It's saying, Lord, you know what's going on. This is me. There is no pretense. I'm as honest as I can be. Sometimes a theme comes out. Then it makes me be quiet and think about something I've just said, and pray about it. For example, maybe

I'm angry. Why? Am I envious of someone? Sometimes the colloquy is like a mini-meditation.

Robert, too, has found his own way of concluding prayer with a colloquy. For him, the colloquy is a time of great openness with God: "I'm as honest as I can be." It is a time of asking and of offering. As with Monica, the colloquy blesses the closing of his prayer.

I Conclude with an Our Father

Ignatius invites us to conclude this colloquy itself with an Our Father. He simply invites us to do this, without further explanation. But one can think of many good reasons for doing so: the Our Father continues and elevates the direct address of the colloquy; it summarizes all prayer, and thus fittingly concludes the colloquy; it is a brief, uniquely rich vocal prayer, which serves as an effective bridge from the time of prayer to what follows.[31]

One woman says:

I always end with an Our Father, just praising God. I end with the "acts" that we learned in my prayer group: adoration, contrition, thanksgiving, and supplication.

Another notes:

I say an Our Father as I end my prayer. Then I make up a prayer to God, through Christ, in the presence of the Holy Spirit. I say, thank you for being with me in this hour. I have a talk with God about what came up during the prayer and thank him for the day.

Yet another says:

I always conclude by thanking God for giving me this time, for the faith he has given me, for whatever grace I received. Sometimes I end with a Glory Be.

With a certain freedom — including, in one case, the substitution of a Glory Be for the Our Father — these people conclude their prayer with a brief vocal prayer.[32] Ignatius's counsel merits our consideration as well.

Reviewing Our Prayer

At this point our prayer is complete. Ignatius offers one final counsel, however, which may greatly assist growth in prayer. He suggests that after our prayer we *review* the experience. After I finish the prayer, he says, "I will look at how it went with me in the contemplation or meditation" (*SpirEx*, 77). This might be done briefly as the prayer is concluding, or, if time permits, after the prayer.

This review *deepens our awareness of the gift* given in the day's prayer. Questions such as these may assist us:

- As I prayed with the Scripture, what was I *thinking?*

- What drew my attention? What struck me?

- As I prayed with the Scripture, what was I *feeling?*

- What stirred in my heart? Did I feel joy?

- Did I experience peace? Was I anxious?

- Did I struggle in any way?[33]

This review also helps us *find our personal way* of praying. Questions such as these may assist us:

- Did this way of preparing help me to pray?
- This time of day? This place?
- Was this way of proceeding during the prayer helpful?

According to what we observe, we may adapt our choices. Gradually, we will find our most effective personal approach to prayer.

Edward relates his experience of the review:

When I make the review, my attentiveness during the prayer is better. I started writing it to help me do it more faithfully. It makes the graces explicit. It's a confirmation of what happened in the prayer. I find that writing the review reinforces the habit of praying attentively.

I usually spend a half hour in my prayer with Scripture. Then I take a break for about five minutes. I put the kettle on for coffee or tea. I don't turn on the television. If I do, I'll get hooked. Then I sit and write at the dining room table. I spend about seven or eight minutes in the review. At times it may be fifteen, depending on what comes out of it. I don't go longer than fifteen minutes.

The review is very valuable for me. Yet, at times, I resist it. Recently that has been the case. I know the review helps me pray if I do it. But recently I've been saying, "I'll do it later," and I wind up doing it several days later. I had to ask myself: Why am I avoiding it? What am I resisting if I get deeper in the prayer? Then I realized that I'm at a shift in my life and my activity, and I was finding it hard to look at this.

I am grateful to Edward for the honesty of his sharing. His words express the richness of the review: "When I make the review, my *attentiveness* during the prayer is better. . . . It makes the graces *explicit*. It is a *confirmation* of what happened in the prayer. . . . The review is very *valuable* for me." His words also indicate that the review may at times require courage. Edward's honest exploration of his resistance brings him to the threshold of spiritual newness — to deeper understanding of his heart in a time of change.[34]

Denise says:

> The key for me is writing things down. Then I can look back at what has happened in my prayer. It's about not forgetting. Then I can talk about it later in spiritual direction.

Like Edward, Denise finds that writing helps her review her prayer. Her comments also add a further consideration of importance: accompaniment on the journey of prayer. These two spiritual means in combination — *personal review* of prayer and *a competent person* with whom to speak about this — greatly assist growth in prayer. We will return to this point in our next chapter.

Anne observes:

> I usually pray for about forty-five minutes to an hour at the end of the day. I end the prayer by writing things down. I open my eyes after the prayer. Sometimes I put on Christian music. Then I start to write — whatever came up from the Scripture.
>
> Something would be missing if I didn't do this. It's also a good practice because, if I encounter certain problems or other situations, and I pray about them, I can go back in my journal and see how God responded to this. It helps a lot.

The benefits of the review are once again evident. Anne knows that the review helps her and that "something would be missing" without it.

Might a similar review assist us in our prayer? Do we have time for it, at least briefly? On occasion, if not regularly? Might the final moments of our time for prayer be dedicated to this review? Might we make this review after the prayer? And would we, like Edward, Denise, and Anne, benefit from such a review? Consideration of such questions may greatly benefit our prayer.

Chapter Seven

Further Counsels for Prayer

She would chew on every single word, and when she found one she especially liked, she would stop for as long as her mind found pleasure grazing there.
— Said of St. Catherine of Siena by a witness

"To Find More Readily What One Desires"

Our review of the outline of meditation and contemplation is now complete. We have seen all of its elements: the body of the prayer and the steps that prepare for and conclude it. In his Spiritual Exercises, however, Ignatius does not simply outline meditation and contemplation. He also supplies what he calls "additions," that is, further counsels "to make the exercises better and to find more readily what one desires" in them (*SpirEx,* 73).

We have already seen some of these; in this chapter we will explore others. We will also explicitly examine several points simply mentioned earlier. We will consider:

> the *body* in prayer,
> the *pace* of our prayer,
> *struggles* in prayer,
> *growth* in prayer,
> *accompaniment* in prayer.

Prayer and the Body

Ignatius mentions the body as prayer begins: "I will stand for the space of an Our Father . . . considering how God our Lord looks upon me, etc., and I will make *a gesture* of reverence or humility" (*SpirEx*, 75). Through this gesture the body expresses what the heart perceives. From the outset, Ignatius involves the *total* person in prayer.

Ignatius also speaks of the body during the prayer: "I will enter the contemplation, now kneeling, now prostrate on the ground, now lying face upwards, now seated, now standing, always intent on seeking what I desire" (*SpirEx*, 76). The options are many. We choose the posture which best helps us *to seek what we desire* in prayer.[35]

Ignatius invites us to review our prayer "either seated, or walking leisurely" (*SpirEx*, 77). Elsewhere he suggests that a person pray "keeping the eyes closed or fixed in one place without allowing them to wander" (*SpirEx*, 252). Such repeated references to the body clearly highlight its importance in prayer.

Brian describes his experience:

> I pray seated in a chair. I need to physically have myself sit up or I will fall asleep. I put my back up against the back of the chair. As I begin, I concentrate on my breathing. I become aware of my breath, and that allows me to relax and be still. When I do, often I can feel my body relax. When I feel that unwinding, then I let go of my distractions. I acknowledge them, and I let them go. Then I ask God to be present, to be with me. Then I pick up the Scripture.

Brian is profoundly aware of the body in prayer. He knows which posture best helps him pray and consciously adopts it. His words express the close link between body and spirit in prayer: once he is physically settled ("when I feel that unwinding"), his heart turns to God ("then I ask God to be present, to be with me").

Wise choices regarding the body will greatly bless our prayer. Experience will teach us which choices best help us to pray.

"There I Will Rest"

At what *pace* should we pray with the Scripture? Should we pray with each verse of the text? Should we focus on a part of it? If so, on which part? What if we do not finish the text?

Ignatius writes: "In the point in which I find what I desire, there I will rest, without anxiety to move forward until I am satisfied" (*SpirEx*, 77). Ignatius's words richly respond to such questions: wherever my heart finds what it desires — communion with God, clarity, love, peace, renewed hope — "*there* I will *rest, without anxiety* to move forward *until I am satisfied.*"[36]

A woman wishes to speak with her friend. She knows that the friend is in one of five rooms in the building. If she knocks at the door of the first room and finds her friend, she knocks at no further doors. She has already found the friend whom she sought. On another day her friend may be in another room. Then the woman will knock at other doors until she finds her friend.

Something similar is true of prayer. Should my heart *find what it desires* in a phrase (meditation) or Gospel moment (contemplation), "there I will rest, without anxiety to move forward until I am satisfied." On another day, other points in this Scripture may touch my heart. Today I need only rest in *this* point where I encounter God.

Kathryn contemplates Jesus' passion for hours, "without anxiety to move forward" until her heart is satisfied. Those hours transform her life. Brian prays for days with a Sunday Gospel, "without anxiety to move forward" until his heart is satisfied. That Gospel blesses his week.

Sheila gives an example of her own "rest":

> Three days ago I prayed with the Gospel where Jesus tells us to be dressed for action and to have our lamps lit, to be ready for the master's coming [Luke 12:35–38]. At first it seemed almost military. Then I realized that I was preparing for the bridegroom. As I prayed, "dressed for action" stood out. "Be dressed for action" means that I have to wear my life in the way God wants. I found myself asking: How do I wear my life, Lord? Where do I put my energy? I want to do so many things. Jesus is saying: Don't scatter your energies. He's telling me that he has something he wants me to do. I need to have my lamp lit, to be ready.
>
> I have prayed with this Gospel for the past three days. It's so rich. There's so much there. I think I will stay with it for a long time.

Sheila prays with the Gospel of the daily Mass. This day, one verse stands out: Jesus' call to be dressed for action, ready with lighted lamps (Luke 12:35). This verse speaks to Sheila's heart; she prays with it for three days, and says, "I think I will stay with it for a long time." In Ignatian terms, in "the point" in which she finds what she desires, there Sheila "rests," "without anxiety to go forward," until her heart is satisfied. Sheila prays with spiritual freedom and wisdom, in accordance with Ignatius's teaching.[37]

Struggles in Prayer

Struggles in prayer, as in life more generally, are a normal part of growth. Often they themselves provide the occasion for such growth. We face them confident that, in God, we will have "strength for everything" (Phil. 4:13).

Some struggles pertain to the beginnings. The pianist, the ballet dancer, and the athlete do not begin as masters in their professions. Persevering practice leads them beyond initial awkwardness to the skill we later admire. Because God's grace respects what is human, something similar generally occurs in prayer.

Lisa says:

When I first started praying with Scripture it was really hard. Ten minutes was all I could do. I'd get a headache. I'd get bored.

I've been doing it for two years now. It depends on the Scripture. When it is speaking to me, to what is happening in my life, I find myself staying longer with it. You want some answers — you want to know what is happening. You feel the Holy Spirit. You feel Jesus talking to you. I find myself thinking of things I never thought of before. I see this experience now in a new way.

Lisa has persevered through the normal struggles of the beginnings. With God's grace, she is progressing solidly in prayer.

Other struggles accompany us beyond the beginnings. These too are normal, and perseverance through them yields rich spiritual fruit.

Robert has prayed with Scripture for six years. He observes:

I have needed to persevere. Some days not much seems to happen when I pray. I might go through three or four days like that, and nothing seems to happen. But I say, Lord, I am going to be there today. And something happens. Sometimes I fall asleep during the prayer. And I say, okay, Lord, I'll be back tomorrow.

I am grateful to God. When I began my practice of praying in the morning six years ago, I asked for the gift of prayer. And God has answered my request.

Robert's words are honest, and they are a valuable contribution to our reflections. He has prayed faithfully through days when "nothing seems to happen," days when he falls asleep, and days when "something happens." But he has always trusted that there was good reason to continue the practice of prayer, and that God was blessing him even during the seemingly dull periods. Through it all, Robert's prayer has been growing, and his heart is grateful.

Reviewing four years of praying with Scripture, Andrew says:

God is always there with his Scripture. He always has something to give me, even in times of desolation and dryness. I can look back now and see the growth through times of dryness. God really was there. Those are moments when it takes faith.

God is at work even when prayer is difficult — "he always has something to give me, even in times of desolation and dryness."[38] And perseverance in such times is a source of blessing: "I can look back now and see the growth through times of dryness." At this point, neither Robert nor Andrew fears such struggles. Both understand them to be part of the life of prayer. They know that these struggles are an occasion of growth. Such realism and confidence will strengthen us in our prayer as well.[39]

In times of struggle, accompaniment by a knowledgeable person may be of great assistance. We will return to this point shortly.

Growth in Prayer

Fidelity in prayer leads to growth in prayer. God's grace blesses our efforts, and prayer deepens. The initial struggles pass. We find our personal way to meditate and contemplate. With joy, we sense that God is giving us growth.

Gerald recalls his own growth in prayer:

Before, when I prayed with Scripture, it was more a reading. I would look at the story, try to piece things together, to make sense of the chronology, and so on. Then I learned about *entering* the Scripture. I made some Ignatian retreats, and I was taught the steps that St. Ignatius teaches.

Before, I had nothing. Now I had a technique, a way. And it worked. Scripture became approachable, more than just a story. Through this, it became more of a relationship with God. The steps helped. They gave me a different perspective in approaching Scripture. Before, no one had explained to me how to pray with Scripture. Now I had some tools. I didn't yet know how to use them the way a master would. I couldn't do master carpentry, so to speak, but I could cut a piece of wood.

It was like wearing a stiff glove. I had been given these tools but had not yet made them my own. At first I would use all of the tools. I realized over time that I didn't need to use each one all the time. I became more aware of the Holy Spirit's guidance, and I could use the tools as the Holy Spirit was prompting me to use them. It became more personal. If, for example, I was prompted by the Spirit to enter a colloquy, I would stay there. I wouldn't feel I had to leave there because I had to get on to the next step. I could stay where the grace was, and go deeper.

I see that this is what St. Ignatius intended — that we use these tools as we need them, as we feel moved by the Holy Spirit. Then they became mine, personal. The stiff glove wasn't stiff any longer.

Gerald experiences the joy of learning to pray with Scripture. Through Ignatius's teaching, he learns to enter the Scripture, and his prayer becomes relational. Initially, however, the steps are like a stiff glove. Through persevering prayer, Gerald finds increasing freedom with these steps: "Then they became mine, personal"; "The stiff glove wasn't stiff any longer." When these two elements combine — solid knowledge of the steps and Spirit-guided freedom in employing them — then, like Gerald, we are growing surely in prayer.

Barbara says:

Each day there is a millimeter of growth. I'm not there yet. It's a slow process. I'm a person who says, *Let's get on with it.* But I've really learned to be patient.

Barbara's experience reflects the normal pattern of growth in prayer. Dramatic moments of grace may occur, and when they do, we are grateful. More often, as Barbara indicates, such growth is gradual. Generally we perceive it more in retrospect than in the moment. If, like Barbara, we pray with patient fidelity, such growth will surely occur. Each day will indeed add its spiritual "millimeter" of growth. Our daily prayer is like a mustard seed (Matt. 13:31–32); God's love gives it a power of growth beyond our imagining.

Elizabeth has prayed with Ignatian contemplation for many years. She says:

Sometimes the prayer can be very dry. I'm more accepting now. Sometimes it is very rich. It's a relationship with God. God is always there, I know. It's like with a friend. Sometimes you feel more present, sometimes less. Now it's more like sitting with God, being with God. Silence is more important to me now, a sense of the wonder and the power. I can't find words. Silence is more in my prayer now.

There is realism in Elizabeth's words: "Sometimes the prayer can be very dry.... Sometimes it is very rich." And there is deepening through years of prayer: "Now it's more like sitting with God, being with God.... Silence is more important to me now, a sense of the wonder and the power."[40] Elizabeth's words speak eloquently of growth in prayer. That growth lies open to us all.

Accompaniment in Prayer

When Kathryn prays with the passion of Jesus, she says, as we saw earlier:

One day in prayer, I stood beneath the cross and sank to the ground at its foot after he had died. I had told Jesus I would not leave him alone, and so I stayed there keeping watch. I kept the cross before my eyes for hours, feeling the sorrow Mary must have felt, as I asked for the courage to stay near the cross. It was at this point that *my retreat director pointed out to me* that perhaps God was bringing together Jesus' experience and my own.

Kathryn's retreat director listens as she describes her prayer. He senses what Kathryn herself is as yet unable to see: the link between Jesus' experience in his passion and her experience seventeen years earlier in the hospital. The director's comment helps Kathryn understand her prayer, and this understanding blesses her profoundly: "In prayer...scenes of *my hospital stay* after my stroke so many years before alternated with scenes of *Jesus' passion* and death.... These cleansing tears began a process of healing... as I began to pray over my 'passion.' "

This is a rich experience of *accompaniment* in prayer. It powerfully illustrates how such accompaniment assists growth in prayer. A knowledgeable person may help us understand our prayer, and so follow where the Lord is leading.[41]

Barbara says:

I began praying with Scripture when I began meeting with my spiritual director. The director would give me passages to pray with according to my needs at the time. I have a goal when I pray with Scripture: my next meeting with my director. I take spiritual direction seriously, and I want to do my part. So I try to pray every night. I do it at least three or four times a week.

For me, spiritual direction is at the heart of my prayer with Scripture. I get the passages from the director. At the next meeting, I talk about my prayer with them.

For Barbara, spiritual direction provided the initial impulse for prayer with Scripture. It now provides sustaining energy for that prayer: "I have a goal when I pray with Scripture: my next meeting with my director." Clearly, this accompaniment is central in Barbara's prayer.

Monica says:

Spiritual direction is an important part of my prayer journey. I value it for a sense of accountability — someone to report to. And for a sense of community. It's so helpful to be able to share prayer experiences with someone. It helps to sustain a prayer life.

For Monica, spiritual direction brings two blessings: a sense of accountability and of community. She has someone "to report to," and someone with whom "to share prayer experiences." This forms a significant part of her journey of prayer.

Mark began praying with Scripture several months ago when he joined a prayer group. He says: "Contemplation is harder for me on my own. It is fruitful, but not as fruitful as when I'm led by another."

Lisa also belongs to a prayer group. She says:

> They taught us how to get in touch with feelings when we pray, and how to imagine the Gospel. I love that they give us a Scripture every week. I read it every day during the week and reflect on it. The Scripture may seem connected to what is happening in the week. We meet once a week and share about the Scripture. You speak about the week, and connect it to the Scripture.

Both Mark and Lisa find group accompaniment of great assistance in their prayer. The group provides a sense of community and a place of sharing in prayer. The group leadership suggests helpful texts for prayer.

Many forms of accompaniment in prayer are available. Regular spiritual direction with a knowledgeable guide is of great value. When regular direction may be difficult, at least occasional direction may be possible. Groups led by spiritually prepared guides may be of great assistance. Retreats offer a further setting for group accompaniment and personal direction. On another level, spouses and friends may encourage each other on the journey of prayer.

Such accompaniment blesses us in many ways. Through it, like Barbara, Mark, and the others, we will be greatly strengthened in our prayer.

Chapter Eight

Putting It All Together:
An Example

Today we understand in the sacred Word what we did not know yesterday; tomorrow we will understand what we do not know today. God has graciously disposed this so that every day we may be nourished.
— St. Gregory the Great

The Elements of a Flexible Whole

Thus far we have seen the individual *elements* of meditation and contemplation. It remains now to see these elements in practice as a flexible *whole*.

As throughout, we will approach this through an example. We will accompany Susan as she prays with Scripture for several days.[42]

The example is necessarily individual. It applies Ignatius's teaching to a specific situation. In so doing, it renders the teaching concrete and suggests practical ways of employing it. At the same time, this is simply one model. Guided by Ignatius's teaching and instructed by experience, those who pray will find their personal paths.

First Day

Susan began praying with Scripture one year ago. Initially she prayed for twenty minutes each morning. Now she prays for a half hour, and occasionally longer if time permits.

Susan prays with the readings from the Mass of the day. Some months ago, she saw a spiritual commentary on the Gospels in a bookstore and liked it. She acquired it and uses it to prepare her daily prayer.

Now it is Wednesday evening. Susan is in her room as the day is ending. Before retiring, she looks at the readings for the following day. The Gospel is the cleansing of the leper (Mark 1:40–45).[43]

Susan reads this Gospel. She is especially drawn to the dialogue between the leper and Jesus: "If you wish, you can make me clean"; "I do will it. Be made clean." She then turns to the commentary. It offers a page and a half on this Gospel. One paragraph in particular strikes her:

> Mosaic law separated lepers as outcasts from the rest of the people and required them to cry out, "Unclean, unclean," when others approached (see Leviticus 13:44–46). The leper who approached Jesus directly was breaking Mosaic law. He must have deeply believed and desperately hoped that Jesus had the ability to heal him, for he said, "If you will, you can make me clean" (Mark 1:40). Not only did the leper know his need, he also had to believe that Jesus was the answer to that need.[44]

This scriptural background gives Susan new insight into the leper's action and Jesus' response. Something gently stirs in her heart as she reads this paragraph. Susan knows that she will return to this in prayer the next day. She then concludes her brief preparation and retires.

Susan rises the following morning and prepares for the day. As she does so, the passage of the leper is quietly present in her heart.

Now Susan is ready to begin her prayer. She lifts her heart to the Lord, aware of Jesus' look of love. She asks Jesus for openness in this prayer. She takes the Scripture and attentively rereads Mark 1:40–45. She also rereads the paragraph in the commentary that spoke to her the preceding evening.

Now she sees the Gospel setting — the place where Jesus and the leper meet. As she enters this scene, she asks Jesus for his healing touch in her life, too.

Susan tries to contemplate the Gospel, but is distracted for some minutes. Then she focuses on the moment when the leper kneels before Jesus. She sees him kneel, she hears his cry for help...and something again gently stirs in her heart. She finds herself saying those same words to Jesus: "If you wish, you can make me clean." The courage of the leper, his willingness to risk so much to approach Jesus, his desperate need, and his great hope all speak to her heart. She asks Jesus to touch the place in her that is afraid, to strengthen her in love, to help her respond fully to him this day.

For some minutes, she is simply there with Jesus. Peace comes into her heart, and the beginning of tears.

She spends the final minutes of her prayer thanking the Lord. She says an Our Father, and quietly rises from her prayer. As she prepares for the activity of the day, Susan continues to dwell on the gift of this prayer. The prayer helps her be attentive to and patient with others throughout the day.

Second Day

It is Thursday evening, the end of a busy day. Susan looks at the readings for the coming day. The Gospel is the healing of the paralytic lowered through the roof (Mark 2:1–12). She reads the passage and the commentary. Though this passage is rich, Susan is drawn to remain with the healing of the leper. She decides to pray again with the same Gospel.

Susan begins her prayer as usual the next morning. Again there are times of distraction, but she is able to enter the passage. The prayer is simpler than the day before. She is just there with Jesus, speaking from her heart: "If you wish, you can make me clean." The words express her deep longing for communion with Jesus. And she hears Jesus reply: "I do will it. Be made clean." The rest of the prayer is spent in this sharing of hearts. She rises, strengthened for the day.

Third Day

On Friday evening, before retiring, Susan again looks at the readings for the following day. This time she is drawn to the First Reading (Heb. 4:12–16), and especially to the final verses: "We do not have a high priest who is unable to sympathize with our weaknesses, but one who has similarly been tested. . . . So let us confidently approach the throne of grace to receive mercy." She decides to pray with these verses, and does so the next morning.

The Following Days

At Mass on Sunday, the Gospel is the encounter of Jesus with the first disciples (John 1:35–42). The homily is focused on Jesus as the "Lamb of God" (John 1:36), and

Susan is drawn by the richness of this title. She decides that she will pray with these words the following morning.

On Monday evening none of the readings particularly draws her. Susan then remembers the Gospel of the paralytic lowered through the roof, and how it had spoken to her a few days earlier. At that time, she had preferred to remain with the healing of the leper. She now decides to pray with the healing of the paralytic the following morning.

In the Creativity of the Spirit

This is a snapshot of Susan's prayer for a few days. She has found her way to pray with Scripture and is growing spiritually through this prayer.

Many questions, however, may be raised.

- How will she pray when the regular pattern of these days is upset?
- When she is tired?
- When struggles with health weigh on prayer?
- When she is traveling?
- When concerns of family or work demand late nights and early rising is more difficult?

Throughout this book we have seen the creative answers of real people in real life. We have seen them pray with Scripture daily, or as often as possible during the week. We have watched them pray in the morning, in the afternoon while the children are at school, or in the evening after work. They have told of praying at home, on the subway commuting to work, or in church. They have described praying with the daily readings for Mass, with each Gospel as a whole, with the Sunday Gospel, or with passages chosen according to the need of the moment. Those who pray will find their own creative answers in the Spirit.

This is also a snapshot of Susan's prayer with Scripture one year after she begins.

- How will she pray a year later?
- Five years later? Ten?
- How is the Lord calling each of us to pray now, at this stage of our spiritual journey? Like Susan? In a different way?

Faithful prayer, review of our experience in prayer, and (when possible) conversation with a knowledgeable person will help us find answers.

Chapter Nine

The Fruits of Prayer

Our fulcrum is God: our lever, prayer — prayer which burns with love. With that we can lift the world!
— St. Thérèse of Lisieux

What Will Happen If I Pray This Way?

In these pages we have heard Kathryn, Robert, Monica, Mark, and many others speak about their prayer. We will listen a final time as these persons describe the *fruit* of their prayer.

Edward has prayed with Scripture for several years. In a time of pain, he sought the help of a spiritual director. The director suggested that he make an Ignatian retreat. Edward says:

> When I made the Ignatian retreat it was a powerful experience. I felt that I had actually met Jesus. It was very moving. I felt that I got to know the Son personally and, through him, the Father.
>
> To experience Jesus as sharing in my woundedness gave me a hope that I would be able to understand him from inside myself. If this could happen in this area of my life, it could happen in other areas too. It touched an inner source of hope that I'd not experienced before. It made me feel hopeful in that I didn't feel helpless about the past. I learned that something can be done about the past, that it can be reshaped, . . . that it can take on new

meaning, that it can become something holy, not just a lost cause. It gave me a new attitude toward my history, and all of history.

Prayer with Scripture is a source of healing for Edward. Through it, he *meets Jesus* and experiences Jesus as sharing his woundedness. Through prayer, Edward finds hope: "I learned that something can be done about the past, that it can be reshaped, that it can become something holy." Prayer lifts his sense of helplessness and gives Edward new meaning in life.

Maria observes:

Through my prayer with Scripture I feel very connected to the liturgical seasons [Advent, Christmas, Lent, Easter, Ordinary Time]. I pray with the readings for Sunday Mass. I read the next Sunday's Gospel on the preceding Monday. I let it be a part of me for the week, so that, on Sunday, the Gospel is already engaged in my life. I've done this for years.

Maria's prayer draws her more deeply into the liturgical seasons and unites her with the Church at prayer. Her prayer also unites the Gospel with her daily life.

Anne began praying with Scripture one year ago. She says:

I read the passage until I get caught on a word. All day long I see this word — on the subway, on the bus, at work.

I'm quite talkative, and, before, I had a hard time listening. I'm more ready to listen now. I'll speak, but, if it's not my turn, I'll be quiet. Before, I was more impulsive in decisions. Now there is more discernment. I'm aware of God speaking to me through Scripture. I'm more at peace now. When little things come up, it's easier for me to say, that's okay, it's not a big deal.

Now I'm trying to see God in all things. Heavy things
don't weigh as much. I have the image of Jesus always
with me, like the prayer when I encountered him when
he was with the children [Matt. 19:13–15].

She adds another blessing, in words we saw earlier:

Ever since that encounter with Jesus and experiencing
that he loves me so much, I feel like I have more love to
give, and I want to make others happy. Before, I would
give to others if they had given to me. Now I'm more
giving.

"Before" and "now": Anne is conscious of the change
since she began to pray with Scripture. Now she is more
ready to listen, is more discerning, has more peace, and is
more aware of Jesus with her. She says, "I feel like I have
more love to give."

Richard has been praying with Scripture for many years.
He says:

Some days, prayer is warm, and I feel God's presence.
But there have been plenty of times of struggle in my
prayer, times when I'm tired or distracted or maybe
feeling burdened by something, and so it's not easy to
pray. Some days, it's hard to even know how to pray,
and all I can do is try the best I can.

Still, I've always known that prayer makes a real dif-
ference in my life, no matter how it goes. I'm more
aware of God, I feel more peace as I go through the
day, and I can smile more. I keep learning that I have a
Savior, that I don't have to make everything happen by
myself. Then the burdens lift for awhile. The most important thing, what I want most and what I still struggle
to accept, is that when I pray I know that I am loved.

When I pray, I have more to give to others. Whatever the struggles might be, I know that prayer is the
most important thing in my life. I wouldn't want to be
without it.

Richard speaks honestly about struggles in prayer. There
are days when he is tired or distracted, and days when "it's
hard to even know how to pray." he is also deeply conscious
of its blessed fruits: He is more aware of God, feels more
peace, can give more, learns that he has a Savior, and, above
all, knows that he is loved. His prayer is the center of his
life: "Whatever the struggles might be, I know that prayer
is the most important thing in my life."

Barbara began praying with Scripture several months ago.
She says:

> I usually find an insight in the Scripture, and I try to
> change my actions in light of that. My tires aren't stuck.
> I see what God wants me to see.
>
> After I pray like this, I'm constantly thinking these
> thoughts. Thoughts can come to me on the subway, on
> the street, or at work. The prayer goes into the day.

Barbara is aware of growth through her prayer. She is
not stuck in one place on the spiritual journey. Gradually,
prayer leads to transformation: "I try to change my actions
in light of that." And, she says, "The prayer *goes into the
day.*" The sign of authentic prayer is here.

Personal encounter with Jesus, new hope, overcoming
of helplessness, healing, union with the Church, greater
discernment, deeper peace, lightening of burdens, greater
awareness of God, experience of Jesus as Savior and of being
loved by God, gradual transformation, more love to give
others: the fruits of prayer are many and rich. They are offered to all by the God who promises, "Ask and it will be

given to you; seek and you will find; knock and the door will be opened to you" (Matt. 7:7).

"A Pure Gift of Grace"

Dan says of his experience of prayer:

> I began praying with Scripture seven years ago. I had a deep desire to grow in love of God. These seven years have transformed me. They've been a pure gift of grace. Praying with Scripture is meeting this awesome, wonderful, good God, who wants all to know that he is searching for them. It's worth it. Like Jacob and all those years of service [Gen. 29].
>
> When I made the Spiritual Exercises, I saw an image of a sheep going over a cliff, and Jesus reaching after it. I wander, I get lost, I am afraid. But the shepherd comes. He's been looking for me all the time. I've never been alone.

Dan's words express the mystery of prayer: the mingling of human effort and divine grace in the transforming power of prayer. There is human effort: "Like Jacob and all those years of *service*." But there is, above all, divine grace: "They've been a *pure gift of grace*." All who pray can say with St. Paul, "I worked . . . though it was not I, but the grace of God which is with me" (1 Cor. 15:10).

Ignatius's methods for prayer assist that human effort. They are a means of *disposing* ourselves to receive the gift of prayer (*SpirEx*, 238). This is our part in prayer: to dispose our hearts, as best we can, to encounter God. Ignatius's methods, with sure knowledge of human nature, assist us in this process.

As we read Dan's words, we stand once again on holy ground. Prayer with Scripture is, indeed, "meeting this awesome, wonderful, good God." It truly is "a pure gift of grace." Prayer does teach us that we are never alone. And through prayer we are transformed so that, as Thérèse says, *we can lift the world.*

Ignatius can guide us, as generations before us, on that journey. Then we will walk with sure steps toward the God whose love ever calls us to new life.

Notes

1. All quotations in this book from the *Spiritual Exercises* are translated by the author from the original Spanish (Autograph version). In translating, I have consulted and occasionally adopted wording from Elder Mullan, S.J., *The Spiritual Exercises of St. Ignatius of Loyola: Translated from the Autograph* (New York: P. J. Kenedy & Sons, 1914), and Louis Puhl, S.J., *The Spiritual Exercises of St. Ignatius Based on Studies in the Language of the Autograph* (Chicago: Loyola University Press, 1951). All emphasis (italicized words) in the quotations is the author's own.

2. The single exception is "Susan" in chapter 8. See note 42.

3. Kathryn James Hermes, F.S.P., *Surviving Depression: A Catholic Approach* (Boston: Pauline Book & Media, 2003), 32. The subsequent quotations are from pp. 32–34. The author describes the background to this prayer on pp. x–xi.

4. *SpirEx*, 45: "The first exercise is meditation with the three powers." These three powers are the *memoria, entendimiento,* and *voluntad:* memory, understanding, and will. Ignatius gives five meditations in the Spiritual Exercises: *SpirEx,* 45–53, 52–61, 65–71, 136–47, 149–56.

5. John Clarke, trans., *Story of a Soul: The Autobiography of Saint Thérèse of Lisieux* (Washington, D.C.: ICS Publications, 1996), 192. The subsequent quotations are taken from pp. 193–95.

6. To emphasize the points under consideration, in this and in the subsequent quotations from Thérèse's text, I have removed her italics and have inserted my own.

7. Ignatius speaks of the successive truths in a Scripture as *points* ("puntos"). For each meditation (and contemplation) he suggests several such points.

8. Ignatius later indicates that we "hear with our [imaginative] hearing what they [the persons in the Gospel event] say *or might say*"

(*SpirEx*, 123). Emphasis added. The words Kathryn hears are of this latter kind. In the Gospel account, Jesus does not use these precise words. They reflect accurately, however, the scriptural witness regarding Jesus (John 10:18–19, Gal. 2:20, etc.): they are, in Ignatius's sense, words that Jesus "might say." Ignatius understands that we have such freedom in imaginative prayer with Gospel events. Its fruitfulness is evident in Kathryn's prayer.

9. Ignatius explicitly mentions such personal participation in contemplation. "I make myself a little poor person and an unworthy slave, observing them [the persons in the grotto after Jesus' birth], contemplating them, and serving them in their needs, as if I were present, with all possible respect and reverence" (*SpirEx*, 114). Here Ignatius clearly indicates that imaginative contemplation is both receptive (observing, contemplating) and active (in the specific setting of Jesus' birth, serving). Both elements are evident in Kathryn's contemplation: she sees, hears, and observes (receptive stance), and personally participates (active stance) in the events.

10. *SpirEx*, 106–9: "ver las personas" (see the persons), "oír lo que hablan" (hear what they say), "mirar lo que hacen" (observe what they do). In *SpirEx*, 114–16, Ignatius describes these three steps more amply: "ver las personas" (see the persons), "mirar, advertir, y contemplar lo que hablan" (observe, note, and contemplate what they say), "mirar y considerer lo que hacen" (observe and consider what they do).

11. In the contemplations of the Incarnation and birth, the *successive exercise* of these *three imaginative activities* (seeing, hearing, observing) constitutes the points (*SpirEx*, 106–8, 114–16). In the fifty contemplations given later (*SpirEx*, 262–312), the *successive elements* of the *Gospel scene* constitute the points — all three imaginative activities (seeing, hearing, observing) are applied to each successive element in the Gospel text. Kathryn takes this latter approach in her contemplation of the passion. Either approach may be followed, though the second is more commonly used.

12. I take these from William Barry's excellent treatment of this question in *God and You: Prayer as a Personal Relationship* (New York: Paulist Press, 1987), 25–26, 45.

13. A theological truth underlies imaginative contemplation. The events of Jesus' life occurred in the past. The *saving power* (grace) of

these events, however, is not limited to a moment in the past: it is offered to all, at all times in history. The annual liturgical cycle is based on this truth. Our liturgical celebration of Christmas, for example, is more than a simple remembrance of a past event. Through our liturgical celebration of Jesus' birth, we have fresh access to the *ever-present* grace of that birth. Imaginative contemplation applies this same truth to personal prayer. When we contemplate Jesus' birth (Luke 2:1–14), we do more than simply recall a past event. Through our contemplation, we have fresh access to the *ever-present* grace of his birth. Our imaginative seeing, hearing, and observing dispose our hearts to receive that grace today. Ignatius's vocabulary itself expresses this truth. He describes the Gospel events we contemplate as "*mysteries* of the life of Christ our Lord" (*SpirEx*, 261). Emphasis added.

14. "People obviously differ in their imaginative abilities, or, perhaps better, in the kinds of imagination they have. Some people seem to be able to visualize in colorful detail the whole gospel scene, almost as though their imaginations were creating a Technicolor movie. Others have a vivid auditory imagination so that whole conversations seem to go on in their heads and hearts. Others, and here I count myself, do not seem to see or hear much at all, but to feel the story and the characters in a way that is hard to describe.... Actually, everyone has an imagination. If you wince when someone describes the impact of a hammer hitting his thumb, you have an imagination; if you can enjoy a good story, you have an imagination. Imaginations differ; we need to let God use the one we have." Barry, *God and You*, 42.

15. When Ignatius describes *meditation*, he invites us to prepare by "seeing with the *imaginative* sight" (*SpirEx*, 47) and speaks of "*imagining* Christ our Lord before me" in the final colloquy (*SpirEx*, 53). When he describes *contemplation*, Ignatius indicates that in each point, after imaginatively seeing, hearing, and observing, the person will "*reflect* to gain some fruit" (*SpirEx*, 106–8, 114–16). Emphasis added.

16. In the *Spiritual Exercises* Ignatius carefully specifies both the place (*SpirEx*, 20) and time (four or five hours each day) of prayer. The same is true of the choice of Scripture and the brief commentary on it offered by the director (*SpirEx*, 2).

17. "After I go to bed, just as I want to go to sleep, for the space of [time it takes to say] a *Hail Mary*, I will think of the hour when I have to rise and for what I am rising, briefly summing up the exercise [the

prayer] which I have to make" (*SpirEx,* 73); "When I waken, without giving place to one thought or another, I will turn my attention at once to that which I am going to contemplate" (*SpirEx,* 74). See also *SpirEx,* 131 and 239.

18. "The faculty which it [prayer] must awaken and turn toward the object of worship — if this term may be used — is not merely that of thought and action, but the inmost *inwardness* of the soul: in other words, the very thing which in man corresponds to the mysterious holiness of God." Romano Guardini, *The Art of Praying: The Principles and Methods of Christian Prayer* (Manchester, N.H.: Sophia Institute Press, 1994), 11.

19. For these steps, see the outlines of meditation and contemplation given on pp. 16 and 17 of this book.

20. Testimony of Diego Laínez, quoted in Charles O'Neill, S.J., "*Acatamiento:* Ignatian Reverence in History and in Contemporary Culture," *Studies in the Spirituality of Jesuits* 8 (1976): 7.

21. See Robert Marsh, S.J., "Looking at God Looking at You: Ignatius' Third Addition," *The Way* 43 (2004): 19–28.

22. "How does 'God our Lord look upon me' as I begin to pray . . . ? If the unseen God is revealed to us in Jesus (John 1:18), then we may rephrase this question as follows: how does *Jesus* look upon those who approach him with humble and sincere hearts? Jesus looks upon Nathaniel and that look tells Nathaniel that he is deeply known and loved; it is a look that changes his life (John 1:48). Jesus sees Levi and his look gives fresh meaning to Levi's existence (Mark 2:14). Jesus sees a woman in tears, and her tears are transformed into the joy of life restored (Luke 7:13). A man approaches Jesus, and the Gospel tells us that 'Jesus, looking at him, loved him' (Mark 10:21). Jesus sees a woman burdened for eighteen years with an illness; she is set free and praises God (Luke 13:12–13). Jesus looks upon Peter in his time of utter failure, a look that leads to tears and to renewal in a love that will never again be shaken (Luke 22:61). All of this may be summarized in the words of John of the Cross: 'the look of God is love and the pouring out of gifts.'" Timothy M. Gallagher, O.M.V., *The Examen Prayer: Ignatian Wisdom for Our Lives Today* (New York: Crossroad, 2006), 124.

23. In the *Spiritual Exercises,* Ignatius places this preparatory prayer at the beginning of every hour of prayer. It is a constantly renewed

prayer for the availability described in the Principle and Foundation (*SpirEx*, 23).

24. Those who desire to make the Spiritual Exercises but whose responsibilities do not permit them to leave home may make the Exercises in daily life over several months. Such persons dedicate an hour a day to prayer with Scripture and meet once a week with the director to discuss their prayer.

25. Ignatius speaks of this as the *historia* (history), or, more amply, "to bring to mind the history of the thing I am to contemplate" (*SpirEx*, 102). This step is not found in the meditations of the First Week, and is found in all the contemplations and meditations (*SpirEx*, 137, 150) of the Second, Third, and Fourth Weeks.

26. Bernard Basset, S.J., *Let's Start Praying Again: Field Work in Meditation* (New York: Herder and Herder, 1972), 116–17.

27. Ignatius includes it in all five meditations given in the Spiritual Exercises: *SpirEx*, 47, 55, 65, 138, 151. Ignatius also provides a "composition" for a prayer not focused on a specific event (*SpirEx*, 232).

28. This is evident not only from their placement (prior to the body of the prayer), but also from Ignatius's vocabulary: *preparatory* prayer, *prelude* (*preámbulo*).

29. From the Latin *colloquium*, conversation.

30. *SpirEx*, 53, 63, 109, 147. On the communion of the saints, see the *Catechism of the Catholic Church*, nos. 946–62.

31. "Ignatius also considers the transition out of the formal time of [prayer]...and into our more habitual activity. Again he does so succinctly, in this case simply mentioning the prayer of the Our Father.... Here as throughout the *Spiritual Exercises* Ignatius suggests that heart-to-heart conversation ('colloquy') with God flow into and conclude with a classic formula of prayer (*SpirEx*, 54, 63, etc.). This brief classic prayer assists in the transition from the quiet communion of formal prayer to the more active space to follow. In this way the formal time of prayer does not end abruptly; rather it concludes gently, respecting our human need for transitional space when our hearts have encountered another person deeply.... The Our Father itself, a prayer that Cyprian tells us is 'overflowing with spiritual strength' and is 'a summary of heavenly teaching' in which 'nothing is omitted that may be found in our prayers and petitions,' may constitute a helpful transition for us. Certainly it is

an exquisitely *relational* way to complete a prayer that is itself so profoundly relational." Gallagher, *The Examen Prayer,* 125. The reference
is to St. Cyprian's "De Dominica Oratione," in *Corpus Christianorum,
Series Latina,* 1976, IIIA, 94.

32. Ignatius mentions two other such prayers in the context of colloquies: the *Anima Christi* (Soul of Christ), and the Hail Mary. *SpirEx,*
63, 147.

33. We touch here upon *discernment of spirits:* becoming aware
of, understanding, and responding wisely to spiritual movements, that
is, to spiritual consolation and desolation, and their related thoughts. I
have discussed this in *The Discernment of Spirits: An Ignatian Guide for
Everyday Living* (New York: Crossroad, 2005), and *Spiritual Consolation: An Ignatian Guide for the Greater Discernment of Spirits* (New
York: Crossroad, 2007).

34. Edward's experience also suggests the value of reviewing our
spiritual experience *during the day.* In Ignatian spirituality, this is the
daily examen prayer. I have discussed this in *The Examen Prayer.*

35. In what he calls the Second Method of Prayer (*SpirEx,* 249–
57), Ignatius counsels the person to pray "kneeling or seated, according
to the greater disposition in which he finds himself and as more devotion
accompanies him" (*SpirEx,* 252). The *Spiritual Exercises* abound in references to the body: the Additions (*SpirEx,* 73–90), the Rules for Eating
(*SpirEx,* 210–17), the Third Method of Prayer (*SpirEx,* 258–60), etc.

36. Ignatius writes that in prayer "it is not much knowledge that
fills and satisfies the soul, but the feeling and tasting of things interiorly"
(*SpirEx,* 2).

37. St. Francis de Sales speaks of considerations that may arise as
we pray, and writes: "If your mind finds enough appeal, light, and fruit
in any of them, remain with that point and do not go any further. Imitate
the bees, who do not leave a flower as long as they can extract any honey
out of it. But if you do not come on anything that appeals to you after
you have examined and tried it for a while, then go on to another, but
proceed calmly and simply in this matter and do not rush yourself."
John Ryan, trans. and ed., *Introduction to the Devout Life* (Garden
City, N.Y.: Image Books, 1959), 84.

38. For Ignatius's counsel regarding prayer in time of desolation, see
SpirEx, 13. On desolation and discernment of spirits more generally, see
note 33.

39. Obviously, much more may be said about difficulties in prayer than space permits here. See, for example, Romano Guardini, *The Art of Praying: The Principles and Methods of Christian Prayer* (Manchester, N.H.: Sophia Institute Press, 1995). Earlier editions of this work were entitled *Prayer in Practice*.

40. Ignatius expects progressive simplification in prayer as the daily pattern of prayer in the Spiritual Exercises indicates (repetitions and application of the senses). Such simplification is strikingly apparent in the Second Week. During the first three days of the Second Week, retreatants dedicate five hours of prayer to *two* Gospel texts; on days five through twelve, they dedicate five hours of prayer to *one* Gospel text (on day ten, this text is simply two verses: *SpirEx,* 161, 288).

41. Ignatius always presumes such accompaniment in his Spiritual Exercises. See especially *SpirEx,* 17.

42. The examples cited thus far have all been taken from the real experience of concrete individuals. This final example, however, is what I might call a "reflected" example, a composite one. The experience is not that of a specific individual, but rather "reflects" the experiences of the many people I have encountered in thirty years of spiritual direction and retreats. In this reflected sense, "Susan" is a very real person.

43. The readings in this example are from the First Week in Ordinary Time, Year 1. The Sunday Gospel is from Year B. The Sunday and weekday readings for Mass are readily available in book form, in monthly publications, and online.

44. Leo Zanchettin, ed., *Mark: A Devotional Commentary: Meditations on the Gospel According to St. Mark* (Ijamsville, Md.: Word Among Us Press, 1998), 32. This is only one of many such books. Commentaries are also available in monthly publications or online. My own *Ignatian Introduction to Prayer: Scriptural Reflections According to the Spiritual Exercises* (New York: Crossroad, 2008) is intended to assist prayer through brief commentaries on scriptural texts.

Also by Timothy Gallagher, O.M.V.

AN IGNATIAN INTRODUCTION TO PRAYER
Scriptural Reflections According to the Spiritual Exercises

Following the spiritual itinerary of the Spiritual Exercises of Ignatius of Loyola, these forty reflections are a wonderful resource for those beginning to pray with scripture. They provide accompaniment in the first, tentative steps of such blessed prayer. For those who already pray with Scripture, and who seek new depth in prayer, these emotionally rich reflections may provide an opportunity for such growth. They are also useful for spiritual directors, retreat directors, small groups in parishes, among friends, and in the home.

"An Ignatian Introduction to Prayer is like a pocket guide to a growing relationship with a loving God — a road map for the pilgrimage. I look forward to using it myself in order to make the road ahead more clear."
— Tim Muldoon, author of *The Ignatian Workout*

978-0-8245-2487-6, paperback

crossroad

Also by Timothy Gallagher, O.M.V.

THE DISCERNMENT OF SPIRITS
An Ignatian Guide for Everyday Living

By providing a sound understanding of Ignatian principles and applying them in a skillful way to daily life, Father Gallagher meets the pressing needs of retreat directors, retreatants, students of spiritual theology, and others interested in deepening their spiritual lives. I know of no comparable volume that proves so helpful.

–Harvey D. Egan, S.J., Professor of Systematic and
Mystical Theology, Boston College
(from the book's foreword)

0-8245-2291-5, paperback

THE EXAMEN PRAYER
Ignatian Wisdom for Our Lives Today

With a foreword by Fr. George Aschenbrenner, S.J.

This is the first book to explain the examen prayer, one of the most popular practices in Christian spirituality. Fr. Timothy Gallagher takes us deep into the prayer, showing that the prayer Ignatius of Loyola believed to be at the center of the spiritual life is just as relevant to our lives today.

Topics include: Desire ~ A Day with Ignatius ~ Gratitude ~ Petition ~ Review ~ Discernment ~ Forgiveness ~ Our Image of God ~ The Future ~ Flexibility ~ The Freedom of the Spirit ~ The Contemplative Capacity ~ Journaling ~ Renewal ~ Courage ~ Spiritual Consolation ~ Letting Go ~ Fruits ~ Discerning Awareness throughout the Day

0-8245-2367-9, paperback

crossroad

Also by Timothy Gallagher, O.M.V.

SPIRITUAL CONSOLATION
An Ignatian Guide for the Greater Discernment of Spirits

"This book presents to committed, busy Christians Ignatius's Second Week Rules for Discernment. Ignatius's teaching here is a treasure that good people desperately need.... Timothy Gallagher writes exceptionally clearly and attractively about these Second Week Rules. His writing is marked by a reverence and love for Ignatius's text, and by a gift for clear exposition. He charts a wise course through the academic discussions, and his footnotes will provide ample guidance for those who want to explore them further. He shows how real people can be helped by what can sound so arcane when you read Ignatius's text straight off. This book is a valuable new contribution to the Ignatian literature, one that I welcome warmly. Read it and learn from it."

— Philip Endean, S.J., Editor, *The Way*

This book is both the completion of Dr. Gallagher's esteemed Ignatian trilogy and a provocative work in its own right.

0-8245-2429-2, paperback

crossroad

Of Related Interest

St. Ignatius Loyola
LETTERS TO WOMEN
Edited and introduced by Hugo Rahner, S.J.

"The written word remains and bears perpetual witness."
— Ignatius of Loyola

"Ignatius of Loyola reveals to us the secret fulness of his heart not only in his Spiritual Exercises, his mystical diary, and his memoirs, but also in his letters, especially in his hitherto almost unknown correspondence with women of his time. We present it for the first time in this book as a complete whole." — Hugo Rahner, S.J., from the foreword

In this volume in the Herder & Herder library of Ignatian Spirituality, Hugo Rahner, influential author and the brother of renowned theologian Karl Rahner, selects the most important letters from Loyola's hand, showing how they illuminate Loyola's spiritual vision in his day and our own. The letters are both inspirational devotions and instructive examples of how we too can strengthen and renew one another in spiritual growth.

With a foreword by Gill K. Goulding, I.B.V.M.

978-0-8245-2475-3, paperback

crossroad

Of Related Interest

Dean Brackley, S.J.
THE CALL TO DISCERNMENT
IN TROUBLED TIMES
*New Perspectives on the Transformative Wisdom
of Ignatius of Loyola*

As the centerpiece of Crossroad's expanding offerings in Jesuit spirituality and thought, we offer this remarkable book from Dean Brackley, a leader in social justice movements and professor in El Salvador. Brackley takes us through the famous Ignatian exercises, showing that they involve not only private religious experience but also a social, moral dimension, including the care for others.

0-8245-2268-0, paperback

Check your local bookstore for availability.
To order directly from the publisher,
please call 1-800-888-4741 for Customer Service
or visit our Web site at *www.CrossroadPublishing.com.*
For catalog orders, please send your request to the address below.

THE CROSSROAD PUBLISHING COMPANY
info@CrossroadPublishing.com

All prices subject to change.

crossroad